FIVE STEPS TO ROMANTIC LOVE

FIVE STEPS TO ROMANTIC LOVE

A Workbook for Readers of
Love Busters and *His Needs, Her Needs*

Willard F. Harley, Jr.

Revell

a division of Baker Publishing Group
www.RevellBooks.com

© 1993, 2002, 2009 by Willard F. Harley, Jr.

Published by Revell
a division of Baker Publishing Group
P.O. Box 6287, Grand Rapids, MI 49516-6287
www.revellbooks.com

New paperback edition published 2009

Printed in the United States of America

Library of Congress Cataloging-in-Publication Data
Harley Willard F.
    Five steps to romantic love : a workbook for readers of love busters and his needs, her needs / Willard F. Harley, Jr.—Updated ed.
        p.   cm.
    ISBN 978-0-8007-3358-2 (pbk.)
    1. Marriage. 2. Communication in marriage. 3. Man-woman relation-ships. I. Title.
HQ734.H284 2009
646.7'8076—dc22   2008053072

15 16   8 7 6

Contents

Introduction

Romantic love can last a lifetime if couples follow two rules: (1) meet each other's most important emotional needs and (2) avoid hurting each other. It's just that simple. I wrote *Love Busters* to help couples follow the first rule: learning to identify and eliminate harmful behavior that I call "Love Busters." I wrote *His Needs, Her Needs* to help couples follow the second rule: learning to identify and meet each other's most important emotional needs.

These two books, *His Needs, Her Needs* and *Love Busters*, contain contracts, questionnaires, inventories, worksheets, and other forms that I use as part of marital therapy. But because of space limitations, they are reduced in size and often incomplete. In response to many of my readers' requests for the full-sized forms, I've compiled this workbook. It contains not only the forms described in my two books but also many others that will help you create and sustain romantic love.

This workbook is not intended to be used by itself: It is a supplement to *His Needs, Her Needs* and *Love Busters*. As the forms are introduced here, I refer you to the chapters in these books that will be helpful in understanding how to use the forms.

Both books have been rewritten. So when you use this workbook be sure you are using the latest editions of the books.

I have grouped these forms into a five-step sequence. The sequence is suggested in the opening chapter of *Love Busters*, but I make it clearer in this workbook.

The first step in building romantic love is to make a commitment to do just that. Goals are not achieved by chance: leaving things to chance creates problems. So if you want to keep romantic love in your marriage, you must commit yourselves to that purpose. I designed the **Agreement to Overcome Love Busters and Meet the Most Important Emotional Needs** form to spell out very clearly what it takes to guarantee romantic love. In essence, this form commits you to following the remaining four steps.

The second step is to identify habits that destroy romantic love. As I explain in the first chapter of *Love Busters*, it's pointless to build romantic love if you persist in habits that undermine your effort. I designed the **Love Busters**

Questionnaire to help you identify these destructive habits. When you and your spouse have accurately completed this questionnaire, you'll know if you've been destroying romantic love.

The third step is to create and execute a plan that eliminates the Love Busters you identified in the second step. Chapters 3–8 in *Love Busters* introduce and describe each of the six Love Busters. They also suggest methods to help you eliminate them. Most of the forms in this section of the workbook are described in these chapters and are designed to help you overcome Love Busters systematically.

There are three forms to help you overcome each Love Buster. First, there is an inventory to identify the bad habits. Then there is a form to document the strategy you've chosen to eliminate them. Finally, a worksheet helps you document progress toward your goal.

When you've conquered Love Busters, you're ready for the fourth step to romantic love: identifying the most important emotional needs. When these needs are met, romantic love is guaranteed. The **Emotional Needs Questionnaire** is designed to help you identify and communicate your most important emotional needs to each other.

The fifth step to romantic love is learning to meet the needs you identified in step four. Chapters 3–12 in *His Needs, Her Needs* describe the ten most common emotional needs and some of the forms I use to help couples learn to meet these needs. These forms and several others I use are printed in this section of the workbook.

The forms in this workbook are arranged in a logical sequence. First, behavior likely to meet each need is identified in an *inventory* form. Second, a plan to learn behavior that meets the need is documented on a *strategy* form. Third, progress toward the achievement of the goal is recorded on a *worksheet* form.

This workbook will help you (1) make a commitment to create and sustain romantic love, (2) identify habits that destroy romantic love, (3) overcome those Love Busters, (4) identify the most important emotional needs, and (5) learn to meet them.

I don't believe in "insight therapy" as an effective way to resolve marital conflict—I believe in "action therapy." Insight is a good beginning, but it's what you do that solves your problem. The forms in this workbook are designed to turn insight into action. They will help you identify your marital problems and create ways to solve them. If you cannot create a strategy that you and your spouse agree to, or if you cannot follow your own program, as evidenced by your failure to complete assignments, then you need a marriage counselor to help guide you. (The last chapter of this workbook will help you find a good counselor.)

Your effort to sustain romantic love will also be an effort to resolve your marital conflicts. That's because most conflicts arise when one spouse tries to gain at the other's expense (a Love Buster) or refuses to meet the other's important emotional needs. The only way romantic love can be sustained is by learning to accommodate each other's feelings, avoiding behavior that hurts each other, and learning behavior that meets each other's needs. When you've learned how to do that, conflicts are resolved and romantic love will be yours for a lifetime.

Follow these *Five Steps to Romantic Love* and you'll have a marriage that is passionate and free of conflict. It's well worth the effort!

Note: You may copy these forms as many times as you like for your personal use in the pursuit of your own marital objectives. In fact, you will need multiple copies of many forms to complete the assignments. However, the forms may not be copied for distribution to others without permission of the publisher.

Making a Commitment to Build Romantic Love

It's a shame that our wedding vows are usually vague or impossible to keep. Wedding vows should state realistic commitments that, if kept, would ensure the success of the marriage. Without clear and attainable objectives, it's no wonder that over half of our marriages end in divorce and another one-third remain disappointing throughout life. That leaves about one marriage in five that is successful. Part of the problem is that we begin marriage without clear objectives.

I've written a marriage contract that should have been used in your wedding. If your vows were vague and gave you no clear direction, don't despair. There's time to make a new commitment that makes more sense. This commitment is designed to help you achieve for your marriage everything you ever hoped for: sustained romantic love. In this contract you and your spouse will commit yourselves to do what it takes to be in love with each other for the rest of your lives.

Romantic love is the feeling of incredible attraction toward another person, and people rarely marry without it. It just doesn't make sense to marry someone unless you're in love. But romantic love is very fragile and requires special care to continue throughout life.

The way I explain the rise and fall of romantic love to my clients is to introduce them to the Love Bank. We all have one inside of us that keeps a record of the way people affect us. When someone does something that makes us feel good, that person deposits love units in our Love Bank. Parents, siblings,

13

children, and most friends deposit love units when they meet our emotional needs, which makes us feel good. We like people who have positive balances in their accounts with us.

When someone meets our *most* important emotional needs, large numbers of love units are deposited because that person makes us feel exceptionally good. When the account in our Love Bank reaches a threshold, say, of 10,000 love units, we experience romantic love toward that person. Generally that threshold can be reached only when a member of the opposite sex meets our most important emotional needs.

Just as in any bank account, deposits are not the only transactions in the Love Bank; withdrawals can also take place. When someone does something that makes us feel bad, that person withdraws love units. If love unit deposits cease and withdrawals continue, an account can become overdrawn. When that happens, we dislike or even come to hate that person.

How we feel toward people depends on their account balances in our Love Bank. When they have very high balances, we like or possibly love them. When they have negative balances, we dislike or possibly hate them.

You must remember that when I talk about romantic love I am referring to *emotional* feelings of attraction. The emotional feelings of love and hate depend on Love Bank balances. But there's another type of love that I call "care," which is meeting someone's needs or taking someone's feelings into account. This kind of love does not necessarily depend on the balances in the Love Bank. It's possible for all of us to love (care for) someone we are not "in love" with, someone we are not emotionally attracted to. Love that implies "care" is a *behavior* that actually meets someone's needs. Romantic love, on the other hand, is a *feeling* we experience when someone meets *our* most important emotional needs.

The two concepts of romantic love and care come together in marriage. You care for your spouse when you meet his or her most important emotional needs. That in turn causes your spouse to feel romantic love for you. Your spouse's care for you, meeting your needs, causes you to feel romantic love for your spouse.

I view romantic love as a litmus test of our ability to care. If we are effective in our care, romantic love is secure, because we are depositing love units and avoiding their withdrawal. We are meeting the most important emotional needs and avoiding harmful behavior. When our spouses no longer feel romantic love toward us, we are failing to care effectively.

The first chapter of *Love Busters* and the first two chapters of *His Needs, Her Needs* provide a more detailed explanation of what I've been writing about. The basic point I make is that if you want romantic love, you must avoid hurting each other, and you must meet each other's most important emotional needs. In other words, you must care for each other.

The marriage contract that I recommend commits you to developing the care that sustains romantic love. Once you develop that care, you'll meet your spouse's most important emotional needs and avoid hurting him/her. In other words, you'll be depositing love units and not withdrawing them. Romantic love is guaranteed!

The first part of this agreement commits you to avoiding Love Busters, habits that cause your spouse unhappiness. My book *Love Busters* is written to help couples learn to overcome these destructive habits. If you have not already read this book, you should read at least the first eight chapters to gain an understanding of Love Busters and the first part of this agreement.

The second part of the agreement commits you to identifying and meeting your spouse's five most important emotional needs. If you have not already read *His Needs, Her Needs*, you should read at least chapters 1, 2, and 14 in that book. Chapter 16 (Building Romantic Love with Care) in *Love Busters* will also provide you with an explanation of this commitment.

The third part of the agreement commits you to setting aside enough time to meet each other's emotional needs. I recommend at least fifteen hours of undivided attention each week to meet the emotional needs of affection, sexual fulfillment, recreational companionship, and conversation. These four emotional needs are certain to be important to you or your spouse, and they cannot be met without a commitment of time. When you were courting, you probably needed that much time to fall in love with each other, and you still need it to stay in love. If you fail to schedule enough time to be together after marriage, all your best efforts to meet each other's needs will fail. It takes time to fall in love and it takes time to stay in love. Chapter 17 (Building Romantic Love with Time) in *Love Busters* explains in more detail why you need undivided attention.

After you have read this agreement and signed it with a witness present, you've completed the first step to romantic love: a commitment to build romantic love. It's also a commitment to complete the remaining four steps.

Agreement to Overcome Love Busters and Meet the Most Important Emotional Needs

THIS AGREEMENT is made this _____ day of _____, 20_____, between _____, hereinafter called "husband," and _____, hereinafter called "wife," whereby it is mutually agreed:

I. The husband and wife agree to avoid being the cause of each other's pain or discomfort by protecting each other from:

A. **Selfish Demands:** Commanding the other to do something with implied threat of punishment if he/she refuses. If selfish demands occur, the husband and wife will follow a course of action that identifies selfish demands, investigates their causes, keeps a record of their occurrences, and replaces them with thoughtful requests.

B. **Disrespectful Judgments:** Attempts to change the other's attitudes, beliefs, and behavior by trying to force his/her way of thinking through lectures, ridicule, threat, or other forceful means. If disrespectful judgments occur, the husband and wife will follow a course of action that identifies disrespectful judgments, investigates their causes, keeps a record of their occurrences, and replaces them with respectful persuasion.

C. **Angry Outbursts:** Deliberate attempts to hurt the other because of anger, usually in the form of verbal or physical attacks. If angry outbursts occur, the husband and wife will follow a course of action that identifies angry outbursts, investigates their motives and causes, keeps a record of their occurrences, and eliminates them.

D. **Dishonesty:** Failure to reveal to the other correct information about emotional reactions, personal history, daily activities, and plans for the future. If dishonesty occurs, the husband and wife will follow a course of action that identifies dishonesty, investigates its causes, records its occurrences, and replaces it with emotional, historical, current, and future honesty.

E. **Annoying Habits:** Behavior repeated without much thought that bothers the other spouse. If an annoying habit occurs, the husband and wife will follow a course of action that identifies the annoying habit, investigates the motives and causes of the habit, keeps a record of its occurrences, and eliminates the habit.

F. **Independent Behavior:** Conduct of one spouse that ignores the interests and feelings of the other. If an independent behavior occurs, a husband and wife will follow a course of action that identifies the independent behavior, investigates its cause, keeps a record of its occurrence, and replaces it with interdependent behavior, conduct that nurtures and protects the interests and feelings of both spouses.

II. The husband and wife agree to meet each other's most important emotional needs by:

A. Identifying each other's emotional needs and selecting at least five that are most important to the husband and at least five that are most important to the wife. These may include any of the following:

1. **Affection:** Expressing love in words, cards, gifts, hugs, kisses, and courtesies, creating an environment that clearly and repeatedly expresses love.

2. **Sexual Fulfillment:** Understanding one's own sexual response and that of the spouse; learning to bring out the best of that response in both oneself and the other so that the sexual relationship is mutually satisfying and enjoyable.

3. **Conversation:** Setting aside time each day to talk to each other about events of the day, feelings, and plans; avoiding angry or judgmental statements or dwelling on past mistakes; showing interest in the spouse's favorite topics of conversation; balancing conversation, using it to inform, investigate, and understand each other; and giving each other undivided attention.

4. **Recreational Companionship:** Developing an interest in the favorite recreational activities of the spouse, learning to be proficient in them, and joining in those activities. If they prove to be unpleasant after an effort has been made, negotiating new recreational activities that are mutually enjoyable.

5. **Honesty and Openness:** Describing one's own positive and negative feelings, events of one's past, daily events and schedule, plans for the future; never leaving the spouse with a false impression; answering the spouse's questions truthfully and completely.

6. **Physical Attractiveness:** Keeping physically fit with diet and exercise; wearing hair and clothing in a way that the spouse finds attractive and tasteful.

7. **Financial Support:** Assuming responsibility to house, feed, and clothe the family at a standard of living acceptable to the spouse, but avoiding working hours and travel that are unacceptable to the spouse.

8. **Domestic Support:** Creating a home environment that offers a refuge from the stresses of life; managing the home and care of the children in a way that encourages the spouse to be in the home enjoying the family.

9. **Family Commitment:** Scheduling sufficient time and energy for the moral and educational development of the children; reading to them and taking them on frequent outings; learning about appropriate child-training methods and discussing those methods with the spouse; avoiding any child-training method or disciplinary action that does not have the enthusiastic support of the spouse.

10. **Admiration:** Understanding and appreciating the spouse more than anyone else; never criticizing but showing profound respect and pride.

B. Creating a plan to help form the new habits that will meet these five needs.

C. Evaluating the success of the plan; creating a new plan if the first is unsuccessful; learning to meet new emotional needs if the spouse replaces any of the original five with new needs.

III. The husband and wife agree to give undivided attention to each other a minimum fifteen hours each week, meeting some of each other's most important marital needs by:

A. Ensuring privacy, planning time together that does not include children, relatives, or friends so that undivided attention is maximized.

B. Using the time to meet the needs of affection, sexual fulfillment, conversation, and recreational companionship.

C. Choosing a number of hours that reflects the quality of marriage: fifteen hours each week if the marriage is mutually satisfying and more time if marital dissatisfaction is reported by either spouse.

D. Scheduling the time together in advance of each week and keeping a permanent record of the time actually spent.

IV. THIS AGREEMENT is being made under, and will be governed by, the laws of the state of _____.

IN WITNESS WHEREOF, the parties hereto have signed this agreement on the day and year first above written:

| _____ | _____ | _____ |
| Husband | Wife | Witness |

Identifying Love Busters

Love Busters are your habits that cause your spouse to be unhappy. Whenever you engage in a Love Buster, you make Love Bank withdrawals.

Why do you engage in Love Busters? Why do you cause your spouse to be unhappy? One of the most important reasons for Love Busters is that, while they may make your spouse feel bad, they make *you* feel good. Most Love Busters gain pleasure for you at your spouse's expense. When your spouse complains about Love Busters, you rationalize your behavior and explain away the fact that you're simply being thoughtless and selfish.

Since your Love Busters usually make you feel good while your spouse feels bad, the one best able to identify them is your spouse. Similarly, you are in the best position to identify your spouse's Love Busters.

I've designed the **Love Busters Questionnaire** to help you identify the Love Busters in your marriage. Two questionnaires are to be completed: one by you and one by your spouse.

Before you complete these questionnaires, you should be familiar with chapters 1–8 in *Love Busters*. You should also try to answer the questions at the end of each chapter.

The analysis of each Love Buster follows a sequence of questions. The first question asks how much unhappiness it causes you. If it doesn't cause you any unhappiness, it's not a Love Buster, and you don't need to answer the remaining questions. But if it causes you unhappiness, your spouse needs to understand how often it happens (question 2), the form(s) that it takes (question 3), the worst form(s) (question 4), when it first started (question 5), and how it has developed over time (question 6).

At the end of the questionnaire, you're asked to rate the Love Busters according to the unhappiness they create. While all Love Busters should be eliminated, it makes sense to work on the most painful Love Busters first.

The results of these questionnaires will help you understand the pain and unhappiness that's created in your marriage. When you cause your spouse emotional pain, you not only withdraw love units, but you encourage your spouse to build emotional defenses that make him/her withdraw from you. Those emotional defenses prevent you from depositing love units to make up for the loss. In other words, when your spouse has withdrawn emotionally from you, he/she won't let you meet his/her emotional needs. It's only when you overcome Love Busters that the emotional barrier is removed and you're in a position to meet your spouse's emotional needs. That's why your Love Busters should be eliminated *before* you learn to meet each other's needs. That's the goal of the third step to romantic love.

Her Love Busters Questionnaire

This questionnaire is to be completed by the *wife*. It's designed to help identify your husband's Love Busters. Your husband engages in a Love Buster whenever one of his habits causes you to be unhappy. By causing your unhappiness, he withdraws love units from his account in your Love Bank, and that, in turn, threatens your romantic love for him.

There are six categories of Love Busters. Each category has its own set of questions in this questionnaire. Answer all the questions as candidly as possible. Do not try to minimize your unhappiness with your spouse's behavior. If your answers require more space, use and attach a separate sheet of paper.

When you have completed this questionnaire, go through it a second time to be certain your answers accurately reflect your feelings. Do not erase your original answers, but cross them out lightly so that your husband can see the corrections and discuss them with you.

The final page of this questionnaire asks you to rank the six Love Busters in order of their importance to you. When you have finished ranking the Love Busters, you may find that your answers to the questions regarding each Love Buster are inconsistent with your final ranking. This inconsistency is common. It often reflects a less than perfect understanding of your feelings. If you notice inconsistencies, discuss them with your husband to help clarify your feelings.

1. **Selfish Demands:** Attempts by your spouse to force you to do something for him, usually with implied threat of punishment if you refuse.

   A. **Selfish Demands as a Cause of Unhappiness:** Indicate how much unhappiness you tend to experience when your spouse makes selfish demands of you.

   ```
   0        1        2        3        4        5        6
   ```
   I experience   I experience   I experience
   no unhappiness   moderate unhappiness   extreme unhappiness

   B. **Frequency of Spouse's Selfish Demands:** Indicate how often your spouse makes selfish demands of you.

   _____ selfish demands each day/week/month/year.
   (write number)   (circle one)

   C. **Form(s) Selfish Demands Take:** When your spouse makes selfish demands of you, what does he typically do?

   _____

   _____

   _____

   D. **Form of Selfish Demands That Causes the Greatest Unhappiness:** Which of the above forms of selfish demands causes you the greatest unhappiness?

   _____

   _____

   _____

   E. **Onset of Selfish Demands:** When did your spouse first make selfish demands of you?

   _____

   _____

   _____

   F. **Development of Selfish Demands:** Have your spouse's selfish demands increased or decreased in intensity and/or frequency since they first began? How do recent selfish demands compare to those of the past?

   _____

   _____

   _____

2. **Disrespectful Judgments:** Attempts by your spouse to change your attitudes, beliefs, and behavior by trying to force you into his way of thinking. If (1) he lectures you instead of respectfully discussing issues, (2) feels that his opinion is superior to yours, (3) talks over you or prevents you from having a chance to explain your position, or (4) ridicules your point of view, he is engaging in disrespectful judgments.

   A. **Disrespectful Judgments as a Cause of Unhappiness:** Indicate how much unhappiness you tend to experience when your spouse engages in disrespectful judgments toward you.

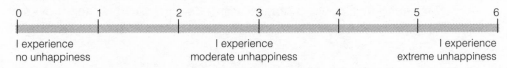

   B. **Frequency of Spouse's Disrespectful Judgments:** Indicate how often your spouse tends to engage in disrespectful judgments toward you.

   _____ disrespectful judgments each day/week/month/year.
   (write number)   (circle one)

   C. **Form(s) Disrespectful Judgments Take:** When your spouse engages in disrespectful judgments toward you, what does he typically do?

   _____

   _____

   D. **Form of Disrespectful Judgments That Causes the Greatest Unhappiness:** Which of the above forms of disrespectful judgments causes you the greatest unhappiness?

   _____

   _____

   E. **Onset of Disrespectful Judgments:** When did your spouse first engage in disrespectful judgments toward you?

   _____

   _____

   F. **Development of Disrespectful Judgments:** Have your spouse's disrespectful judgments increased or decreased in intensity and/or frequency since they first began? How do recent disrespectful judgments compare to those of the past?

   _____

   _____

3. **Angry Outbursts:** Deliberate attempts by your spouse to hurt you because of anger toward you. They are usually in the form of verbal or physical attacks.

   A. **Angry Outbursts as a Cause of Unhappiness:** Indicate how much unhappiness you tend to experience when your spouse attacks you with an angry outburst.

0	1	2	3	4	5	6

I experience   I experience   I experience
no unhappiness   moderate unhappiness   extreme unhappiness

   B. **Frequency of Spouse's Angry Outbursts:** Indicate how often your spouse tends to engage in angry outbursts toward you.

      _____ angry outbursts each day/week/month/ year.
   (write number)   (circle one)

   C. **Form(s) Angry Outbursts Take:** When your spouse engages in angry outbursts toward you, what does he typically do?

     _____

     _____

     _____

   D. **Form of Angry Outbursts That Causes the Greatest Unhappiness:** Which of the above forms of angry outbursts causes you the greatest unhappiness?

     _____

     _____

     _____

   E. **Onset of Angry Outbursts:** When did your spouse first engage in angry outbursts toward you?

     _____

     _____

     _____

   F. **Development of Angry Outbursts:** Have your spouse's angry outbursts increased or decreased in intensity and/or frequency since they first began? How do recent angry outbursts compare to those of the past?

     _____

     _____

     _____

4. **Dishonesty:** Failure of your spouse to reveal his thoughts, feelings, habits, likes, dislikes, personal history, daily activities, and plans for the future. Dishonesty is not only providing false information about any of the above topics, but it is also leaving you with what he knows is a false impression.

A. **Dishonesty as a Cause of Unhappiness:** Indicate how much unhappiness you tend to experience when your spouse is dishonest with you.

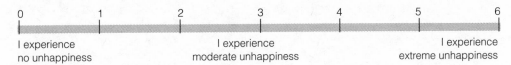

| 0 | 1 | 2 | 3 | 4 | 5 | 6 |

I experience
no unhappiness

I experience
moderate unhappiness

I experience
extreme unhappiness

B. **Frequency of Spouse's Dishonesty:** Indicate how often your spouse tends to be dishonest with you.

_____ instances of dishonesty each day/week/month/year.
(write number)   (circle one)

C. **Form(s) Dishonesty Takes:** When your spouse is dishonest with you, what does he typically do?

_____

_____

_____

D. **Form of Dishonesty That Causes the Greatest Unhappiness:** Which of the above forms of dishonesty causes you the greatest unhappiness?

_____

_____

_____

E. **Onset of Dishonesty:** When was your spouse first dishonest with you?

_____

_____

_____

F. **Development of Dishonesty:** Has your spouse's dishonesty increased or decreased in intensity and/or frequency since it first began? How do recent instances of dishonesty compare to those of the past?

_____

_____

_____

5. **Annoying Habits:** Behavior repeated by your spouse without much thought that bothers you. These habits include personal mannerisms such as the way your spouse eats, cleans up after himself, and talks.

A. **Annoying Habits as a Cause of Unhappiness:** Indicate how much unhappiness you tend to experience when your spouse engages in annoying habits.

```
  0         1         2         3         4         5         6
  |_____|_____|_____|_____|_____|_____|
I experience              I experience              I experience
no unhappiness          moderate unhappiness      extreme unhappiness
```

B. **Frequency of Spouse's Annoying Habits:** Indicate how often your spouse tends to engage in annoying habits.

_____ occurrences of annoying habits each day/week/month/year.

(write number)   (circle one)

C. **Form(s) Annoying Habits Takes:** When your spouse engages in annoying habits toward you, what does he typically do?

_____

_____

_____

D. **Form of Annoying Habits That Causes the Greatest Unhappiness:** Which of the above forms of annoying habits causes you the greatest unhappiness?

_____

_____

_____

E. **Onset of Annoying Habits:** When did your spouse first engage in annoying habits?

_____

_____

_____

F. **Development of Annoying Habits:** Have your spouse's annoying habits increased or decreased in intensity and/or frequency since they first began? How do those recent annoying habits compare to those of the past?

_____

_____

_____

6. **Independent Behavior:** Behavior conceived and executed by your spouse without consideration of your feelings. These behaviors are usually scheduled and require thought to complete, such as attending sporting events or engaging in a personal exercise program.

A. **Independent Behavior as a Cause of Unhappiness:** Indicate how much unhappiness you tend to experience when your spouse engages in independent behavior.

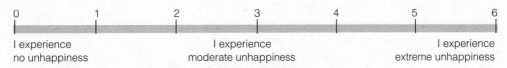

| 0 | 1 | 2 | 3 | 4 | 5 | 6 |

I experience
no unhappiness

I experience
moderate unhappiness

I experience
extreme unhappiness

B. **Frequency of Spouse's Independent Behavior:** Indicate how often your spouse tends to engage in independent behavior.

_____ occurrences of independent behavior each day/week/month/year.
(write number)   (circle one)

C. **Form(s) Independent Behavior Takes:** When your spouse engages in independent behavior toward you, what does he typically do?

_____

_____

_____

D. **Form of Independent Behavior That Causes the Greatest Unhappiness:** Which of the above forms of independent behavior causes you the greatest unhappiness?

_____

_____

_____

E. **Onset of Independent Behavior:** When did your spouse first engage in independent behavior?

_____

_____

_____

F. **Development of Independent Behavior:** Has your spouse's independent behavior increased or decreased in intensity and/or frequency since it first began? How does recent independent behavior compare to that of the past?

_____

_____

_____

Ranking His Love Busters

The six basic categories of Love Busters are listed below. There is also space for you to add other categories of Love Busters that you feel contribute to your marital unhappiness. In the space provided in front of each Love Buster, write a number from 1 to 6 that ranks its relative contribution to your unhappiness. Write a 1 before the Love Buster that causes you the greatest unhappiness, a 2 before the one causing the next greatest unhappiness, and so on, until you have ranked all six.

_____ Selfish Demands

_____ Disrespectful Judgments

_____ Angry Outbursts

_____ Dishonesty

_____ Annoying Behavior

_____ Independent Behavior

_____ _____

_____ _____

His Love Busters Questionnaire

This questionnaire is to be completed by the *husband*. It's designed to help identify your wife's Love Busters. Your wife engages in a Love Buster whenever one of her habits causes you to be unhappy. By causing your unhappiness, she withdraws love units from her account in your Love Bank, and that, in turn, threatens your romantic love for her.

There are six categories of Love Busters. Each category has its own set of questions in this questionnaire. Answer all the questions as candidly as possible. Do not try to minimize your unhappiness with your wife's behavior. If your answers require more space, use and attach a separate sheet of paper.

When you have completed this questionnaire, go through it a second time to be certain your answers accurately reflect your feelings. Do not erase your original answers, but cross them out lightly so that your wife can see the corrections and discuss them with you.

The final page of this questionnaire asks you to rank the six Love Busters in order of their importance to you. When you have finished ranking the Love Busters, you may find that your answers to the questions regarding each Love Buster are inconsistent with your final ranking. This inconsistency is common. It often reflects a less than perfect understanding of your feelings. If you notice inconsistencies, discuss them with your wife to help clarify your feelings.

1. **Selfish Demands:** Attempts by your spouse to force you to do something for her, usually with implied threat of punishment if you refuse.

   A. **Selfish Demands as a Cause of Unhappiness:** Indicate how much unhappiness you tend to experience when your spouse makes selfish demands of you.

   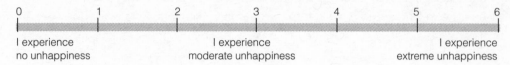

   B. **Frequency of Spouse's Selfish Demands:** Indicate how often your spouse makes selfish demands of you.

   _____ selfish demands each day/week/month/year.
   (write number)   (circle one)

   C. **Form(s) Selfish Demands Take:** When your spouse makes selfish demands of you, what does she typically do?

   _____

   _____

   _____

   D. **Form of Selfish Demands That Causes the Greatest Unhappiness:** Which of the above forms of selfish demands causes you the greatest unhappiness?

   _____

   _____

   _____

   E. **Onset of Selfish Demands:** When did your spouse first make selfish demands of you?

   _____

   _____

   _____

   F. **Development of Selfish Demands:** Have your spouse's selfish demands increased or decreased in intensity and/or frequency since they first began? How do recent selfish demands compare to those of the past?

   _____

   _____

   _____

2. **Disrespectful Judgments:** Attempts by your spouse to change your attitudes, beliefs, and behavior by trying to force you into her way of thinking. If (1) she lectures you instead of respectfully discussing issues, (2) feels that her opinion is superior to yours, (3) talks over you or prevents you from having a chance to explain your position, or (4) ridicules your point of view, she is engaging in disrespectful judgments.

A. **Disrespectful Judgments as a Cause of Unhappiness:** Indicate how much unhappiness you tend to experience when your spouse engages in disrespectful judgments toward you.

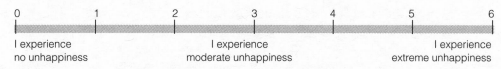

| 0 | 1 | 2 | 3 | 4 | 5 | 6 |

I experience
no unhappiness   I experience
moderate unhappiness   I experience
extreme unhappiness

B. **Frequency of Spouse's Disrespectful Judgments:** Indicate how often your spouse tends to engage in disrespectful judgments toward you.

_____ disrespectful judgments each day/week/month/year.
(write number)   (circle one)

C. **Form(s) Disrespectful Judgments Take:** When your spouse engages in disrespectful judgments toward you, what does she typically do?

_____

_____

_____

D. **Form of Disrespectful Judgments That Causes the Greatest Unhappiness:** Which of the above forms of disrespectful judgments causes you the greatest unhappiness?

_____

_____

_____

E. **Onset of Disrespectful Judgments:** When did your spouse first engage in disrespectful judgments toward you?

_____

_____

F. **Development of Disrespectful Judgments:** Have your spouse's disrespectful judgments increased or decreased in intensity and/or frequency since they first began? How do recent disrespectful judgments compare to those of the past?

_____

_____

3. **Angry Outbursts:** Deliberate attempts by your spouse to hurt you because of anger toward you. They are usually in the form of verbal or physical attacks.

A. **Angry Outbursts as a Cause of Unhappiness:** Indicate how much unhappiness you tend to experience when your spouse attacks you with an angry outburst.

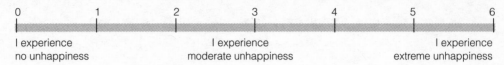

| 0 | 1 | 2 | 3 | 4 | 5 | 6 |

I experience
no unhappiness

I experience
moderate unhappiness

I experience
extreme unhappiness

B. **Frequency of Spouse's Angry Outbursts:** Indicate how often your spouse tends to engage in angry outbursts toward you.

_____ angry outbursts each day/week/month/year.
(write number)   (circle one)

C. **Form(s) Angry Outbursts Take:** When your spouse engages in angry outbursts toward you, what does she typically do?

_____

_____

_____

D. **Form of Angry Outbursts That Causes the Greatest Unhappiness:** Which of the above forms of angry outbursts causes you the greatest unhappiness?

_____

_____

_____

E. **Onset of Angry Outbursts:** When did your spouse first engage in angry outbursts toward you?

_____

_____

_____

F. **Development of Angry Outbursts:** Have your spouse's angry outbursts increased or decreased in intensity and/or frequency since they first began? How do recent angry outbursts compare to those of the past?

_____

_____

_____

4. **Dishonesty:** Failure of your spouse to reveal her thoughts, feelings, habits, likes, dislikes, personal history, daily activities, and plans for the future. Dishonesty is not only providing false information about any of the above topics, but it is also leaving you with what she knows is a false impression.

   A. **Dishonesty as a Cause of Unhappiness:** Indicate how much unhappiness you tend to experience when your spouse is dishonest with you.

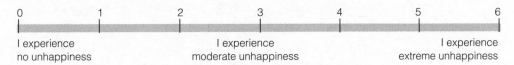

I experience no unhappiness   I experience moderate unhappiness   I experience extreme unhappiness

   B. **Frequency of Spouse's Dishonesty:** Indicate how often your spouse tends to be dishonest with you.

       _____ instances of dishonesty each day/week/month/year.
       (write number)   (circle one)

   C. **Form(s) Dishonesty Takes:** When your spouse is dishonest with you, what does she typically do?

     _____

     _____

     _____

   D. **Form of Dishonesty That Causes the Greatest Unhappiness:** Which of the above forms of dishonesty causes you the greatest unhappiness?

     _____

     _____

     _____

   E. **Onset of Dishonesty:** When was your spouse first dishonest with you?

     _____

     _____

     _____

   F. **Development of Dishonesty:** Has your spouse's dishonesty increased or decreased in intensity and/or frequency since it first began? How do recent instances of dishonesty compare to those of the past?

     _____

     _____

     _____

5. **Annoying Habits:** Behavior repeated by your spouse without much thought that bothers you. These habits include personal mannerisms such as the way your spouse eats, cleans up after herself, and talks.

   A. **Annoying Habits as a Cause of Unhappiness:** Indicate how much unhappiness you tend to experience when your spouse engages in annoying habits.

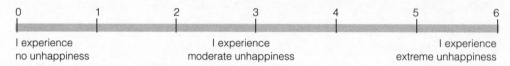

   B. **Frequency of Spouse's Annoying Habits:** Indicate how often your spouse tends to engage in annoying habits.

     _____ occurrences of annoying habits each day/week/month/year.
     (write number)   (circle one)

   C. **Form(s) Annoying Habits Takes:** When your spouse engages in annoying habits toward you, what does she typically do?

    _____

    _____

    _____

   D. **Form of Annoying Habits That Causes the Greatest Unhappiness:** Which of the above forms of annoying habits causes you the greatest unhappiness?

    _____

    _____

    _____

   E. **Onset of Annoying Habits:** When did your spouse first engage in annoying habits?

    _____

    _____

    _____

   F. **Development of Annoying Habits:** Have your spouse's annoying habits increased or decreased in intensity and/or frequency since they first began? How do recent annoying habits compare to those of the past?

    _____

    _____

    _____

6. **Independent Behavior:** Behavior conceived and executed by your spouse without consideration of your feelings. These behaviors are usually scheduled and require thought to complete, such as attending sporting events or engaging in a personal exercise program.

  A. **Independent Behavior as a Cause of Unhappiness:** Indicate how much unhappiness you tend to experience when your spouse engages in independent behavior.

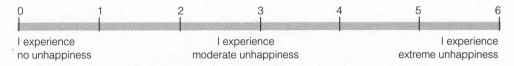

  B. **Frequency of Spouse's Independent Behavior:** Indicate how often your spouse tends to engage in independent behavior.

  _____ occurrences of independent behavior each day/week/month/year.
  (write number)   (circle one)

  C. **Form(s) Independent Behavior Takes:** When your spouse engages in independent behavior toward you, what does she typically do?

  _____

  _____

  _____

  D. **Form of Independent Behavior That Causes the Greatest Unhappiness:** Which of the above forms of independent behavior causes you the greatest unhappiness?

  _____

  _____

  _____

  E. **Onset of Independent Behavior:** When did your spouse first engage in independent behavior?

  _____

  _____

  _____

  F. **Development of Independent Behavior:** Has your spouse's independent behavior increased or decreased in intensity and/or frequency since it first began? How does recent independent behavior compare to that of the past?

  _____

  _____

Ranking Her Love Busters

The six basic categories of Love Busters are listed below. There is also space for you to add other categories of Love Busters that you feel contribute to your marital unhappiness. In the space provided in front of each Love Buster, write a number from 1 to 6 that ranks its relative contribution to your unhappiness. Write a 1 before the Love Buster that causes you the greatest unhappiness, a 2 before the one causing the next greatest unhappiness, and so on, until you have ranked all six.

_____ Selfish Demands

_____ Disrespectful Judgments

_____ Angry Outbursts

_____ Dishonesty

_____ Annoying Behavior

_____ Independent Behavior

_____ _____

_____ _____

Overcoming Love Busters

In your campaign to secure romantic love, you're ready to get down to business if you've completed the first two of the five steps. But first, let's review what you've already accomplished.

The first step committed you to overcoming Love Busters and learning to meet your spouse's most important needs. You completed that step when you signed the Agreement to Overcome Love Busters and Meet the Most Important Emotional Needs.

The second step identified your Love Busters, habits that are destroying romantic love in your marriage. These were identified when you and your spouse completed the Love Busters Questionnaire.

Now you're ready for the third step to romantic love: eliminating those Love Busters that you and your spouse identified. Your Love Buster that is rated highest by your spouse (causes your spouse the most pain) should be your highest priority to overcome. But, eventually, you should eliminate them all.

I've provided forms to help you overcome each Love Buster. Many of these are described in Love Busters, but some are new. In each series of forms, the first is an inventory. It helps you define the Love Buster and investigate its causes and effects. The second is a strategy form that helps you document your plan for overcoming the Love Buster. The third form is a worksheet that you can use to document progress you make in completing your plan. It should eventually show you that you've been successful in defeating the Love Buster.

The rule that should guide you is: Avoid any behavior that causes your spouse pain or discomfort. Whenever our habits are at our spouse's expense, they're also at the expense of romantic love.

Overcoming Selfish Demands

Selfish demands are misguided efforts to resolve marital conflicts. They might work in the short run, getting you what you need today, but they fail to work in the long run. They make your spouse less likely in the future to give you what you demand now. So remember that fact whenever you are tempted to make a demand: If what you want is important to you, never demand it.

But you've tried asking politely, and that hasn't worked. Demands seem to be the only remaining option. Besides, your demand is not unreasonable and if your spouse were thinking clearly, you'd both be in agreement, right? That may all be true, but demands are still misguided. They don't solve problems long-term. All they do is destroy your spouse's love for you. Whatever it is you hope to gain by making a demand, you will lose in love units.

Chapter 3 in *Love Busters* explains how you can overcome making destructive selfish demands. The **Selfish Demands Inventory** was designed to identify the effect and the nature of selfish demands, each spouse's effort to control such demands, and each one's willingness to stop making them. The questions provide an opportunity to reflect on your own habit and that of your spouse to make selfish demands.

The best way to overcome your selfish demands is to learn to replace them with thoughtful requests. I've included a form, **Strategy to Replace Selfish Demands with Thoughtful Requests**, to help you document your plan. It doesn't explain how to make thoughtful requests. That's covered in the next inventory I'll describe. All it does is help you plan the elimination of selfish demands, and encourage you to make thoughtful requests in their place.

So, how should you make a thoughtful request? And can the thoughtful request really achieve your objectives? To help you get what you need from each other, I introduced Basic Concept #10: The Four Guidelines to Successful Negotiation in Marriage (pp. 58–63). This roadmap to marital problem solving shows you how to make thoughtful requests. The first guideline is to make your request safe and cheerful. The second guideline is to explain what you would like and ask your spouse how he or she would feel fulfilling your request. If your spouse indicates that there is a problem with your request, withdraw it in its present form and follow the third guideline, which is to brainstorm alternatives that would be mutually acceptable. The fourth guideline is to keep brainstorming until you find a solution that meets the conditions of the Policy of Joint Agreement (never do anything without an enthusiastic agreement between you and your spouse).

To help you follow the **Four Guidelines to Successful Negotiation** when you make thoughtful requests, use the **Guidelines to Making Thoughtful Requests Inventory**. To help you get into the habit of making thoughtful requests the right way, make multiple copies of this inventory, and follow its guidance whenever you are tempted to make a demand.

To help you document your progress in changing demands into requests, your spouse should complete the **Selfish Demands Worksheet** and the **Thoughtful Requests Worksheet**. Over time, you'll find instances of selfish demands eliminated and instances of thoughtful requests taking their place.

Note: You may need multiple copies of these forms, so be sure to photocopy them rather than writing in the book.

Selfish Demands Inventory

Please answer the following questions. Your answer to the part of each question that refers to your spouse should reflect your best guess without asking directly for the answer.

1. What are the most important reasons that (A) you make demands of your spouse? (B) your spouse makes demands of you?

   A _____

   _____

   B _____

   _____

2. (A) When you make demands of your spouse, how do you usually do it? (B) When your spouse makes demands of you, how does he/she usually go about it?

   A _____

   _____

   B _____

   _____

3. (A) When you make demands of your spouse, how does it make him/her feel? (B) When your spouse makes demands of you, how does it make you feel?

   A _____

   _____

   B _____

   _____

4. (A) When do you try to avoid making demands of your spouse, and how do you do it? (B) When does your spouse try to avoid making demands of you, and how does he/she do it?

   A _____

   _____

   B _____

   _____

5. If you were to decide that you would never make another demand of your spouse, would you be able to stop? Why or why not?

_____

_____

_____

_____

_____

_____

6. Are you willing to stop making demands of your spouse? Why or why not?

_____

_____

_____

_____

_____

_____

7. Please add any further information that might help you and your spouse avoid making demands of each other in the future.

_____

_____

_____

_____

_____

_____

Strategy to Replace Selfish Demands
with Thoughtful Requests

This worksheet is designed to help you create a strategy to replace selfish demands with thoughtful requests. Complete each section of the worksheet to provide yourself with documentation of the process you used to select a strategy.

1. Describe your selfish demands. Include a description of your feelings, your thoughts and attitudes, and the way you make selfish demands of your spouse.

_____

_____

_____

_____

2. Describe the conditions that seem to trigger your selfish demands. Include physical setting, people present, behavior of those people, and any other relevant conditions.

_____

_____

_____

_____

3. What changes in the conditions described in question 2 would help you replace selfish demands with thoughtful requests?

_____

_____

_____

_____

4. Which of the changes described in question 3 can be made with your spouse's enthusiastic support and agreement?

_____

_____

_____

_____

5. Describe your plan to change these conditions. Include a deadline to make the change complete. Be certain the plan has your spouse's enthusiastic support.

_____

_____

_____

_____

6. Which of the changes described in question 3 cannot be made without your spouse's enthusiastic support and agreement or cannot be made at all?

_____

_____

_____

_____

7. Describe your plan to replace selfish demands with thoughtful requests when the conditions described in question 6 exist. Include a deadline for successful completion of the plan. Be certain that the plan has your spouse's enthusiastic support and agreement.

_____

_____

_____

_____

8. How will you measure the success of your plan to replace selfish demands with thoughtful requests? Does this measure of success have your spouse's enthusiastic support?

_____

_____

_____

_____

9. If your plan does not succeed within your designated time limit, will you agree to make a commitment to your spouse to seek professional help in designing an effective plan to protect him/her from your selfish demands? How will you go about finding that help?

_____

_____

_____

_____

Guidelines to Making Thoughtful Requests Inventory

Describe your request:

_____

_____

_____

_____

Guideline #1: *Make your request safe and pleasant*: (1) Be pleasant and cheerful, (2) do not make demands, show disrespect, or become angry, (3) if your reach an impasse, or if you or your spouse makes demands, shows disrespect, or becomes angry, drop the subject and come back to the issue later.

Guideline #2: *What are both of your perspectives*: How would your spouse feel about fulfilling your request? If your spouse agrees enthusiastically to fulfill it, your negotiations are over. If your spouse expresses reluctance, withdraw your request. What are the issues that stand in your spouse's way?

_____

_____

_____

_____

What is your perspective? Why was this request important to you?

_____

_____

_____

_____

Guideline #3: *Brainstorm with abandon*: How could your request have been fulfilled by your spouse in a way that addresses the issues that were raised? Write down every possibility, and then discuss its pros and cons with each other.

_____

_____

_____

_____

Guideline #4: *Choose a way for your spouse to fulfill your request with mutual and enthusiastic agreement*: Keep brainstorming until you have successfully addressed the issues raised by your spouse. Under what conditions is your spouse enthusiastic about fulfilling your request and you are enthusiastic about the way it's fulfilled? Whatever you eventually agree to is likely to be repeated almost effortlessly in the future. So it's well worth the trouble you went to in finding it. What is your final decision?

_____

_____

_____

_____

_____

_____

_____

_____

Selfish Demands Worksheet

Please list all instances of your spouse's selfish demands. These are orders to obey a directive without willingness to accept no for an answer. Failure to comply with a selfish demand usually causes threatened or actual punishment.

	Day	Date	Time	Type of Selfish Demand and Circumstances
1.	_____	_____	_____	_____
2.	_____	_____	_____	_____
3.	_____	_____	_____	_____
4.	_____	_____	_____	_____
5.	_____	_____	_____	_____
6.	_____	_____	_____	_____
7.	_____	_____	_____	_____
8.	_____	_____	_____	_____

Thoughtful Requests Worksheet

Please list all instances of your spouse's thoughtful requests. These are requests for assistance that take your feelings into account. They reflect a willingness to accept no for an answer without resentment or threat of punishment.

	Day	Date	Time	Type of Thoughtful Request and Circumstances
1.	_____	_____	_____	_____
2.	_____	_____	_____	_____
3.	_____	_____	_____	_____
4.	_____	_____	_____	_____
5.	_____	_____	_____	_____
6.	_____	_____	_____	_____
7.	_____	_____	_____	_____
8.	_____	_____	_____	_____

Overcoming Disrespectful Judgments

A disrespectful judgment occurs whenever someone tries to impose a system of values and beliefs on someone else. A spouse who tries to force his/her point of view on the other partner is just asking for trouble. Chapter 4 in Love Busters explains how this bad habit can make you very unattractive.

If you have identified this Love Buster in your marriage, you first need to understand how and why disrespectful judgments persist. The **Disrespectful Judgments Inventory** is designed to identify the effect of disrespectful judgments, their nature, each spouse's effort to control them, and each one's willingness to stop disrespectful judgments. Answers to the questions provide insight regarding your own disrespect as well as that of your spouse.

I've found that one way to avoid disrespectful judgments is to replace them with respectful persuasion. To help you create this plan, use the form **Strategy to Replace Disrespectful Judgments with Respectful Persuasion**. It encourages you to look at, and try to change, environmental conditions that seem to trigger disrespectful judgments.

I suggest a plan to replace disrespectful judgments with respectful persuasion on pages 79–84 in *Love Busters*. This plan can be used as an answer to question 7 in the strategy form. The first step to respectful persuasion is learning to state clearly your opinion *and the opinion of your spouse with respect and understanding*. The second step is explaining how your opinion is in *your spouse's* best interest. The third step is suggesting a test of your opinion to prove that it's in your spouse's best interest. You should be willing to be proven wrong and to consider adopting your spouse's opinion if it turns out that the test fails.

If all of this sounds complicated, remember that the search for and communication of truth is complicated. If you think you have a corner on truth, you will probably be disrespectful of your spouse's alternative views and cause your marriage great harm. You won't convince your spouse if you try to cram your position down his/her throat. But you can be convincing if you show that it's in your spouse's best interest to give your opinion a try.

You may be able to create other strategies that are simpler or more effective in overcoming disrespectful judgments. I encourage you to try anything that you think might work. Whatever it is, be sure to document your plan clearly so that there's no confusion.

Use the **Disrespectful Judgments Worksheet** and **Respectful Persuasion Worksheet** to document your progress toward replacing disrespectful judgments with respectful persuasion. Whenever attitudes or opinions are in conflict, there's a risk of losing love units by trying to impose your unwelcome opinion—or there's an opportunity to learn and grow from each other's reservoir of experience. The first choice is disrespectful and risks romantic love. The second choice improves your wisdom and strengthens romantic love.

Note: You may need multiple copies of these forms, so be sure to photocopy them rather than writing in the book.

Disrespectful Judgments Inventory

Please answer the following questions. Your answer to the part of each question that refers to your spouse should reflect your best guess without asking directly for the answer.

1. What are the most important reasons that (A) you make disrespectful judgments about your spouse? (B) your spouse makes disrespectful judgments about you?

   A _____

   _____

   B _____

   _____

2. (A) When you make disrespectful judgments about your spouse, what do you typically do? (B) When your spouse makes disrespectful judgments about you, what does he/she typically do?

   A _____

   _____

   B _____

   _____

3. (A) When you make disrespectful judgments about your spouse, what hurts your spouse the most? (B) When your spouse makes disrespectful judgments about you, what hurts you the most?

   A _____

   _____

   B _____

   _____

4. (A) When do you try to control disrespectful judgments about your spouse, and how do you do it? (B) When does your spouse try to control disrespectful judgments about you, and how does he/she do it?

   A _____

   _____

   B _____

   _____

5. If you were to decide that you would never make another disrespectful judgment about your spouse, would you be able to stop? Why or why not?

_____

_____

_____

_____

_____

_____

6. Are you willing to stop making disrespectful judgments about your spouse? Why or why not?

_____

_____

_____

_____

_____

_____

7. Please add any further information that might help you and your spouse avoid disrespectful judgments in the future.

_____

_____

_____

_____

_____

_____

Strategy to Replace Disrespectful Judgments with Respectful Persuasion

This worksheet is designed to help you create a strategy to replace disrespectful judgments with respectful persuasion. Complete each section of the worksheet to provide yourself with documentation of the process you used to select a strategy.

1. Describe your disrespectful judgments. Include a description of your feelings, your thoughts and attitudes, and the way you make disrespectful judgments.

   _____

   _____

   _____

   _____

2. Describe the conditions that seem to trigger your disrespectful judgments. Include physical setting, people present, behavior of those people, and any other relevant conditions.

   _____

   _____

   _____

   _____

3. What changes in the conditions described in question 2 would help you replace disrespectful judgments with respectful persuasion?

   _____

   _____

   _____

   _____

4. Which of the changes described in question 3 can be made with your spouse's enthusiastic support and agreement?

   _____

   _____

   _____

   _____

5. Describe your plan to change these conditions. Include a deadline to make the change complete. Be certain the plan has your spouse's enthusiastic support.

_____

_____

_____

_____

6. Which of the changes described in question 3 cannot be made without your spouse's enthusiastic support and agreement or cannot be made at all?

_____

_____

_____

_____

7. Describe your plan to replace disrespectful judgments with respectful persuasion when the conditions described in question 6 exist. Include a deadline for successful completion of the plan. Be certain that the plan has your spouse's enthusiastic support and agreement.

_____

_____

_____

_____

8. How will you measure the success of your plan to replace disrespectful judgments with respectful persuasion? Does this measure of success have your spouse's enthusiastic support?

_____

_____

_____

_____

9. If your plan does not succeed within your designated time limit, will you agree to make a commitment to your spouse to seek professional help in designing an effective plan to protect him/her from your disrespectful judgments? How will you go about finding that help?

_____

_____

_____

Guidelines to Respectful Persuasion Inventory

Describe your opinion:

_____

_____

_____

_____

Guideline #1: *Make your discussion safe and pleasant*: (1) Be pleasant and cheerful, (2) do not make demands, show disrespect, or become angry, (3) if your reach an impasse, or if you or your spouse makes demands, shows disrespect, or becomes angry, drop the subject and come back to the issue later.

Guideline #2: *Express your conflicting opinions to each other with respect and understanding*: What is your spouse's opinion, and how does it differ from yours?

_____

_____

_____

_____

Guideline #3: *Explain how your opinion might be in your spouse's best interest and brainstorm ways to test the value of your opinion*: How could you demonstrate the value of your opinion to your spouse with a test? And give your spouse a chance to test the value of his or her opinion to you.

_____

_____

_____

_____

Guideline #4: If your spouse agrees enthusiastically to your opinion, based on the results of your test, you have achieved respectful persuasion. If the test fails to persuade, go back and brainstorm a new test, or drop the subject. What was the result of your test? Was it convincing? If not, will you return to brainstorming or drop the subject for now?

_____

_____

_____

_____

Disrespectful Judgments Worksheet

Please list all instances of your spouse's disrespectful judgments of your attitudes or opinions. These include lectures, reprimands, belittlements, or other ways that show your point of view is not being respected.

	Day	Date	Time	Type of Disrespectful Judgement and Circumstances
1.	_____	_____	_____	_____
				_____
				_____
2.	_____	_____	_____	_____
				_____
				_____
3.	_____	_____	_____	_____
				_____
				_____
4.	_____	_____	_____	_____
				_____
				_____
5.	_____	_____	_____	_____
				_____
				_____
6.	_____	_____	_____	_____
				_____
				_____
7.	_____	_____	_____	_____
				_____
				_____
8.	_____	_____	_____	_____
				_____
				_____

Respectful Persuasion Worksheet

Please list all instances of your spouse's respectful persuasion. These include instances where you both discuss a differing viewpoint and your spouse makes an effort to persuade you of his/her point of view. Respectful persuasion is never in the form of lectures, reprimands, belittlements, or other ways that would indicate disrespect for your judgment or perspective.

	Day	Date	Time	Type of Respectful Persuasion and Circumstances
1.	_____	_____	_____	_____
				_____
				_____
				_____
2.	_____	_____	_____	_____
				_____
				_____
				_____
3.	_____	_____	_____	_____
				_____
				_____
				_____
4.	_____	_____	_____	_____
				_____
				_____
				_____
5.	_____	_____	_____	_____
				_____
				_____
				_____
6.	_____	_____	_____	_____
				_____
				_____
				_____
7.	_____	_____	_____	_____
				_____
				_____
				_____
8.	_____	_____	_____	_____
				_____
				_____
				_____

Overcoming Angry Outbursts

I encourage you to have absolutely no tolerance for angry outbursts. They make problem solving in marriage impossible, and they destroy your love for each other. You need no other reasons to completely eliminate them once and for all. But there is one other reason to seriously consider: They can lead to permanent disability or even death.

The first step in my plan to help couples overcome angry outbursts is to acknowledge the fact that you, and only you, determine if you have an angry outburst. No one "makes" you angry. If you don't accept that fact, you will never learn to control your temper.

You have already taken the second step, identifying instances of your angry outbursts and their effects, when you completed the **Love Busters Questionnaire**. If either of you identified angry outbursts as a Love Buster in your marriage, you're ready for the third step, understanding why your angry outbursts take place. The **Angry Outbursts Inventory** provides an opportunity for you to reflect on what you might be able to do to control this Love Buster.

The forth step is to create a strategy to avoid conditions to tend to trigger angry outbursts. Questions 1 through 5 in **Strategy to Overcome Angry Outbursts** will document your strategy. Sometimes, all it takes is to make a few lifestyle changes that your spouse would enthusiastically support, like having orange juice for breakfast in the morning (raise blood sugar levels), or driving home from work when there's less traffic.

But in most cases, it's not that simple. If you cannot change the conditions that trigger your angry outbursts, then you need to follow the fifth step, training yourself to control your temper when you cannot avoid frustrating situations. Questions 6 through 9 in **Strategy to Overcome Angry Outbursts** will document that training strategy. Pages 97–112 in my book, *Love Busters*, describe the strategy that I recommend most.

The sixth step is to measure your progress using the **Angry Outbursts Worksheet**. It provides a way to document progress toward their elimination. Since the one with the angry outbursts often forgets details of the episode (and sometimes forgets it altogether), the spouse that had to endure the outburst is the best witness, and his or her memory of it should be taken as the most reliable. If there is serious disagreement regarding the details of outbursts, a counselor specializing in anger management should be consulted.

Continue to document instances of angry outbursts for the rest of your lives together, and hopefully, after a few weeks of practice, there will be nothing to record. If an angry outburst does occur after you thought you had overcome them for good, don't be discouraged. Simply return to your strategy to overcome them, and nip it in the bud before it gains a foothold.

Use good judgment in determining if the anger problems in your marriage can be safely treated by yourselves in the privacy of your home. Sometimes angry outbursts are too dangerous to try to overcome without professional, supervised help. And it might be too dangerous to live together as you are trying to overcome angry outbursts. If your spouse ever hits you in anger, it's safe to conclude that the problem is beyond the reach of unsupervised treatment. Report any incident of physical violence to the police immediately, and request an order of protection while deciding on the best treatment plan. Angry outbursts that are limited to verbal attacks are bad enough. But as I mentioned above, when they become physical, they can lead to permanent disability and even death. Remember, when you are having an angry outburst, you are temporarily insane.

Note: You may need multiple copies of these forms, so be sure to photocopy them rather than writing in the book.

Angry Outbursts Inventory

Please answer the following questions. Your answer to the part of each question that refers to your spouse should reflect your best guess without asking him/her for the answer.

1. What are the most important reasons that (A) you use angry outbursts to punish your spouse? (B) your spouse directs angry outbursts toward you?

   A _____

   _____

   B _____

   _____

2. (A) When you use angry outbursts to punish your spouse, what do you typically do? (B) When your spouse uses angry outbursts to punish you, what does he/she typically do?

   A _____

   _____

   B _____

   _____

3. (A) When you use angry outbursts to punish your spouse, what hurts your spouse the most? (B) When your spouse uses angry outbursts to punish you, what hurts you the most?

   A _____

   _____

   B _____

   _____

4. (A) After you use angry outbursts to punish your spouse, do you usually feel better about the situation than before you used them? Why or why not? (B) When your spouse uses angry outbursts to punish you, does he/she usually feel better about the situation than before he/she used them?

   A _____

   _____

   B _____

   _____

5. (A) Do you feel that punishment evens the score, and that without it your spouse wins and you lose? Explain. (B) Does your spouse feel that punishment evens the score, and that without it you win and he/she loses? Explain.

A _____

_____

B _____

_____

6. (A) When do you try to control angry outbursts toward your spouse, and how do you do it? (B) When does your spouse try to control angry outbursts toward you, and how does he/she do it?

A _____

_____

B _____

_____

7. If you were to decide that you would never direct another angry outburst toward your spouse, would you be able to stop? Why or why not?

_____

_____

_____

_____

8. Are you willing to stop directing angry outbursts toward your spouse? Why or why not?

_____

_____

_____

_____

9. Please add any further information that might help you and your spouse avoid angry outbursts in the future.

_____

_____

_____

_____

Strategy to Overcome Angry Outbursts

. . . .

This worksheet is designed to help you create a strategy to overcome angry outbursts. Complete each section of the worksheet to provide yourself with documentation of the process you used to select a strategy.

. . . .

1. Describe your angry outbursts. Include a description of your feelings of anger, your thoughts and attitudes, and your verbal and physical displays of anger.

   _____

   _____

   _____

   _____

2. Describe the conditions that seem to trigger your angry outbursts. Include physical setting, people present, behavior of those people, and any other relevant conditions.

   _____

   _____

   _____

   _____

3. What changes in the conditions described in question 2 would help you avoid angry outbursts?

   _____

   _____

   _____

   _____

4. Which of the changes described in question 3 can be made with your spouse's enthusiastic support and agreement?

   _____

   _____

   _____

   _____

5. Describe your plan to change these conditions. Include a deadline to make the change complete. Be certain the plan has your spouse's enthusiastic support.

_____

_____

_____

_____

6. Which of the changes described in question 3 cannot be made without your spouse's enthusiastic support and agreement or cannot be made at all?

_____

_____

_____

_____

_____

7. Describe your plan to overcome angry outbursts when the conditions described in question 6 exist. Include a deadline for successful completion of the plan. Be certain that the plan has your spouse's enthusiastic support and agreement.

_____

_____

_____

_____

_____

8. How will you measure the success of your plan to overcome angry outbursts? Does this measure of success have your spouse's enthusiastic support?

_____

_____

_____

_____

_____

9. If your plan does not succeed within your designated time limit, will you agree to make a commitment to your spouse to seek professional help in designing an effective plan to protect him/her from your angry outbursts? How will you go about finding that help?

_____

_____

_____

Angry Outbursts Worksheet

Please list all instances of your spouse's angry outbursts and other acts that you consider punishment for something you did. These include verbal and physical acts of anger and threatened acts of anger toward you, cursing you, and making disrespectful or belittling comments about you.

	Day	Date	Time	Type of Angry Outburst and Circumstances
1.	_____	_____	_____	_____
2.	_____	_____	_____	_____
3.	_____	_____	_____	_____
4.	_____	_____	_____	_____
5.	_____	_____	_____	_____
6.	_____	_____	_____	_____
7.	_____	_____	_____	_____
8.	_____	_____	_____	_____

Overcoming Dishonesty

The Rule of Honesty that I define in *Love Busters* is as follows: *Reveal to your spouse as much information about yourself as you know: your thoughts, feelings, habits, likes, dislikes, personal history, daily activities, and plans for the future.* Dishonesty is the failure to keep any part of this Rule of Honesty.

To help explain this rule, I break it down into four parts:

1. **Emotional honesty:** Reveal your emotional reactions, both positive and negative, to the events of your life, particularly to your spouse's behavior.

2. **Historical honesty:** Reveal information about your personal history, particularly events that demonstrate personal weakness or failure.

3. **Current honesty:** Reveal information about the events of your day. Provide your spouse with a calendar of your activities, with special emphasis on those that may affect your spouse.

4. **Future honesty:** Reveal your thoughts and plans regarding future activities and objectives.

My approach to overcoming dishonesty follows the same logical sequence that I use to eliminate other Love Busters. First, you need to understand how and why dishonesty has established itself in your marriage. The **Dishonesty Inventory** is designed to identify the effect and the nature of dishonesty, each spouse's effort to control it, and each one's willingness to stop being dishonest. The questions provide an opportunity to reflect on your own dishonesty as well as the dishonesty of your spouse.

As you complete the **Dishonesty Inventory**, reflect on the four parts of the Rule of Honesty. You may wish to complete a separate **Dishonesty Inventory** for *each* of the four parts of honesty. Simply make four copies of the form and use one copy for each part. Remember, you're free to make as many copies of the forms in this workbook as you can use in your marriage.

A plan to help you overcome dishonesty is the next step. The **Strategy to Overcome Dishonesty** form will help you describe your plan. In chapter 6 of *Love Busters* I describe four types of liars. Each type requires a different strategy.

The "I'll avoid trouble" liar is usually faced with two problems: He's gotten in trouble and he lies about it. The "getting in trouble" part is usually a result of failing to follow the Policy of Joint Agreement: *Never do anything without the enthusiastic agreement of your spouse.* In other words he does something that he knows will bother his wife if she ever finds out about it. This is an example of independent behavior. By consulting with her first, revising his plan to meet with her approval, and then proceeding, he would avoid having anything to lie about. In most cases, a strategy to overcome this form of lying also should include a strategy to overcome independent behavior.

I've witnessed an increase in people's unwillingness to abandon activities that bother their spouses. Such stubbornness is undoubtedly a major cause for the loss of romantic love. What seems to follow that unwillingness is a new ethic that says it's cruel to expose your spouse to information about yourself that will cause pain. Some say that if you ever do anything that would hurt your spouse, you should keep it to yourself. In other words, dishonesty is on the rise and is seen by some to be ethical.

That's not only the position of the "I'll avoid trouble" liar; it's also the position of the "protector" liar. This type of liar, however, is not necessarily engaged in activities that bother his spouse. He lies to her simply because he feels she is not emotionally adequate to handle the disappointments of life. He thinks she needs protection. A commitment to be honest can sometimes put an end to that myth. He often dislikes being dishonest but hides the truth because he feels it's the right thing to do. This person can learn to be honest overnight as soon as he realizes that his honesty is her best protection.

The "try to look good" liar is usually faced with a deep-seated conviction that what he is or does is not enough to gain admiration. So he thinks lies help gain the acceptance and admiration he so deeply craves. A strategy to overcome this type of lying usually involve a compensating effort to meet the profound need for admiration. (See chapter 7 in *His Needs, Her Needs*.)

The fourth type of liar, the "born" liar, has such serious problems with the truth that I know of no strategy that has overcome this Love Buster. Thankfully, few born liars ever marry.

Once you have created a plan to overcome dishonesty, use the **Dishonesty Worksheet** to measure progress toward its elimination. Normally the worksheet is completed by the spouse who is the victim of the Love Buster. But in this case, it's completed by both spouses together. That's because each spouse has little way of knowing if the other is being honest. The worksheet itself requires honesty.

Note: You may need multiple copies of these forms, so be sure to photocopy them rather than writing in the book.

Dishonesty Inventory

Please answer the following questions. Your answer to the part of each question that refers to your spouse should reflect your best guess without asking directly for the answer.

1. (A) When you are dishonest with your spouse, what kind of liar are you? (B) When your spouse is dishonest with you, what kind of liar do you think he or she is? (circle as many as are appropriate)

   A avoid-trouble liar   protector liar   trying-to-look-good liar   born liar

   B avoid-trouble liar   protector liar   trying-to-look-good liar   born liar

2. (A) When you are dishonest with your spouse, what do you tend to lie about?
   (B) When your spouse is dishonest with you, what do you think he/she tends to lie about? (circle as many as are appropriate)

   A emotional reactions   past history   present activities   future plans

   B emotional reactions   past history   present activities   future plans

3. What are the most important reasons that (A) you are dishonest with your spouse? (B) your spouse is dishonest with you?

   A _____

      _____

   B _____

      _____

4. (A) When you are dishonest with your spouse, what do you typically do? (B) When your spouse is dishonest with you, what does he/she typically do?

   A _____

      _____

   B _____

      _____

5. (A) When you are dishonest with your spouse, what hurts your spouse the most? (B) When your spouse is dishonest with you, what hurts you the most?

   A _____

      _____

   B _____

      _____

6. (A) When do you try to overcome dishonesty with your spouse, and how do you do it? (B) When does your spouse try to overcome dishonesty with you, and how does he/she do it?

A _____

_____

B _____

_____

7. If you were to decide that you would never again be dishonest with your spouse, would you be able to stop? Why or why not?

_____

_____

_____

_____

_____

_____

8. Are you willing to stop being dishonest with your spouse? Why or why not?

_____

_____

_____

_____

_____

_____

9. Please add any further information that might help you and your spouse avoid dishonesty in the future.

_____

_____

_____

_____

_____

_____

_____

Strategy to Overcome Dishonesty

This worksheet is designed to help you create a strategy to overcome dishonesty. Complete each section of the worksheet to provide yourself with documentation of the process you used to select a strategy.

1. Describe your dishonesty. Include a description of your feelings, your thoughts and attitudes, and the way you are dishonest. Which category of dishonesty describes it best (emotional, historical, present, future, complete)?

   _____

   _____

   _____

   _____

   _____

2. Describe the conditions that seem to trigger your dishonesty. Include physical setting, people present, behavior of those people, and any other relevant conditions.

   _____

   _____

   _____

   _____

   _____

3. What changes in the conditions described in question 2 would help you avoid your dishonesty?

   _____

   _____

   _____

   _____

   _____

4. Which of the changes described in question 3 can be made with your spouse's enthusiastic support and agreement?

   _____

   _____

   _____

   _____

5. Describe your plan to change these conditions. Include a deadline to make the change complete. Be certain the plan has your spouse's enthusiastic support.

_____

_____

_____

_____

6. Which of the changes described in question 3 cannot be made without your spouse's enthusiastic support and agreement or cannot be made at all?

_____

_____

_____

_____

7. Describe your plan to overcome dishonesty when the conditions described in question 6 exist. Include a deadline for successful completion of the plan. Be certain that the plan has your spouse's enthusiastic support and agreement.

_____

_____

_____

_____

8. How will you measure the success of your plan to overcome dishonesty? Does this measure of success have your spouse's enthusiastic support?

_____

_____

_____

_____

9. If your plan does not succeed within your designated time limit, will you agree to make a commitment to your spouse to seek professional help in designing an effective plan to protect him/her from your dishonesty? How will you go about finding that help?

_____

_____

_____

_____

Dishonesty Worksheet

Please list all instances of your dishonesty. Generally, you complete the worksheets regarding your spouse's Love Busters, and your spouse does so for yours. But in this case, you and your spouse should complete the worksheet together, since there may be instances of your dishonesty that your spouse would not know of if you did not tell him/her, and vice versa.

	Day	Date	Time	Description and Type of Dishonesty and Circumstances
1.	_____	_____	_____	_____
2.	_____	_____	_____	_____
3.	_____	_____	_____	_____
4.	_____	_____	_____	_____
5.	_____	_____	_____	_____
6.	_____	_____	_____	_____
7.	_____	_____	_____	_____
8.	_____	_____	_____	_____

Overcoming Annoying Habits

Annoying habits are common in marriage. At first, the annoyed spouse usually makes an effort to express how thoughtless the behavior is. When this approach to overcoming the Love Buster is met with anger or indifference, the annoyed spouse eventually gives up trying, and the annoying spouse becomes increasingly difficult to tolerate. Annoying habits may not seem serious to others who don't have to live with them, but for many who do, it's the primary reason that romantic love has been lost.

There are so many reasons for annoying habits. "It's just the way I am." "You're annoyed because you don't like me."

Whatever the excuse, annoying habits can be eliminated without changing your personality, and your spouse will like you a lot more after they're eliminated.

In chapter 7 of *Love Busters*, I suggest that the first step in overcoming annoying habits is to identify them. The **Annoying Habits Inventory: Part 1** helps identify the presence of annoying habits in marriage. This inventory is to be completed by your spouse. The inventory not only lists the annoying habits but also indicates how annoying each one is to a spouse.

A list of annoying habits usually includes a few habits that can be easily overcome with a simple decision to stop doing them. These are usually new habits that have not been hard-wired into your brain, or habits that do not provide much gratification. The second step in overcoming annoying habits is to check off these easy-to-overcome habits from your spouse's list. Of course, if you find that you cannot simply stop doing them with a simple decision to do so, re-enter them on the list.

You are now left with a list of annoying habits that cannot be eliminated with a simple decision. These annoying habits will take special planning and effort on your part to eliminate. The third step in overcoming annoying habits is to select the three most annoying habits from this list to be eliminated first.

The fourth step I recommend is to understand the background and nature of the three annoying habits you have selected. Each habit is analyzed separately by using the **Annoying Habits Inventory: Part 2**. When the analysis is complete, you will have a fairly good idea of how you should attack the problem.

The fifth step is to "get rid of it." The **Strategy to Overcome Annoying Habit**s form will help you document your plan for eliminating each annoying habit. Once you have created a plan to overcome each of the three annoying habits, the **Annoying Habits Worksheet** can be used by your spouse to measure progress toward overcoming these habits, which is the sixth step.

When those three annoying habits are eliminated, the seventh step is to go back to the original list of annoying habits, select three new habits to eliminate, and repeat steps 4, 5, and 6 with those habits.

The mistake that most couples make when they try to eliminate annoying habits is to assume that their willingness to change will solve the problem. Those of us who are in the business of changing behavior know that, in many cases, willingness is essential, but it's only the first step. Once a plan for change is implemented, the target behavior must be carefully monitored by the **Annoying Habits Worksheet**. The worksheet will tell you whether or not your plan is working. If the behavior is not eliminated in a reasonable time, you should create and implement a new plan.

For some, this may seem to be a never-ending exercise in self-torment, but as it turns out, it's a relatively painless way to create compatibility with your spouse. As your annoying habits are eliminated, you'll find that you are much easier to live with and that you haven't lost any of your personality or reason to live. In fact, you'll find that pleasing your spouse becomes increasingly effortless.

Note: You may need multiple copies of these forms, so be sure to photocopy them rather than writing in the book.

Annoying Habits Inventory: Part 1

Annoying habits are behaviors repeated without much thought that bother the other spouse. They include personal mannerisms, such as the way you eat, the way you clean up after yourself (or don't!), and the way you talk.

Please list habits of your spouse that you find annoying: (1) Name the habit, (2) describe it, (3) indicate the frequency with which it occurs, and (4) use a number from 0 to 10 to indicate the intensity at which you find it annoying (0 = not at all annoying, 10 = extremely annoying).

1. Name of habit: _____

   Description of habit: _____

   _____

   Frequency: _____ Intensity: _____

2. Name of habit: _____

   Description of habit: _____

   _____

   Frequency: _____ Intensity: _____

3. Name of habit: _____

   Description of habit: _____

   _____

   Frequency: _____ Intensity: _____

4. Name of habit: _____

   Description of habit: _____

   _____

   Frequency: _____ Intensity: _____

5. Name of habit: _____

   Description of habit: _____

   _____

   Frequency: _____ Intensity: _____

Annoying Habits Inventory: Part 2

This questionnaire is to be completed by the spouse with the annoying habit(s)

· ·

All of the following questions apply to this annoying habit: _____

· ·

1. When did you begin to engage in this habit?

   _____

2. What are the most important reasons you began to engage in this habit?

   _____

   _____

3. What are the most important reasons you engage in this habit now?

   _____

   _____

4. When you engage in this habit, how do you feel?

   _____

5. When you engage in this habit, how does your spouse feel?

   _____

6. Have you ever tried to avoid this habit?_____ If so, how did you do it?

   _____

   _____

7. If you decided to avoid this habit entirely, would you be successful?_____
   Why or why not?

   _____

8. Are you willing to avoid this habit?_____

9. If you have any suggestions that would make elimination of this habit more likely,
   please write them on a separate sheet of paper and attach it to this form.

Strategy to Overcome Annoying Habits

This questionnaire is to be completed by the spouse with the annoying habit

• •

This worksheet is designed to help you overcome the annoying habit of _____.
Complete each section of the worksheet to provide yourself with documentation of the process you used to select a strategy.

• •

1. Describe the annoying habit. Describe the habit itself, what it is that makes it annoying to your spouse, and your feelings, thoughts, and attitudes when you engage in this habit.

   _____

   _____

   _____

   _____

   _____

   _____

2. Describe the conditions that seem to trigger this annoying habit. Include physical setting, people present, behavior of those people, and any other relevant conditions.

   _____

   _____

   _____

   _____

   _____

   _____

3. What changes in the conditions described in question 2 would help you avoid the annoying habit?

   _____

   _____

   _____

   _____

   _____

   _____

4. Which of the changes described in question 3 can be made with your spouse's enthusiastic support and agreement?

_____

_____

_____

_____

_____

_____

5. Describe your plan to change these conditions. Include a deadline to make the change complete. Be certain the plan has your spouse's enthusiastic support.

_____

_____

_____

_____

_____

_____

6. Which of the changes described in question 3 cannot be made without your spouse's enthusiastic support and agreement or cannot be made at all?

_____

_____

_____

_____

_____

_____

7. Describe your plan to overcome the annoying habit when the conditions described in question 6 exist. Include a deadline for successful completion of the plan. Be certain that the plan has your spouse's enthusiastic support and agreement.

_____

_____

_____

_____

_____

_____

8. How will you measure the success of your plan to overcome the annoying habit? Does this measure of success have your spouse's enthusiastic support?

_____

_____

_____

_____

_____

_____

9. If your plan does not succeed within your designated time limit, will you agree to make a commitment to your spouse to seek professional help in designing an effective plan to protect him/her from this annoying habit? How will you go about finding that help?

_____

_____

_____

_____

_____

_____

Annoying Habits Worksheet

* This questionnaire is to be completed by the spouse annoyed by the habit(s)

• •

This worksheet applies to the following annoying habit: _____

    Please list all instances of your spouse's annoying habit. If your spouse negotiated a compromise with you, indicate whether or not you found the compromise annoying.

• •

Day	Date	Time	Circumstances
1. _____	_____	_____	_____
2. _____	_____	_____	_____
3. _____	_____	_____	_____
4. _____	_____	_____	_____
5. _____	_____	_____	_____
6. _____	_____	_____	_____
7. _____	_____	_____	_____
8. _____	_____	_____	_____

Overcoming Independent Behavior

Once you are married, almost everything you decide to do has either a positive or a negative impact on each other—you are either depositing or withdrawing love units with every decision you make. So if your decisions are not made with each other's interests in mind, you will risk destroying the love you have for each other.

I define independent behavior as the conduct of one spouse that ignores the feelings and interests of the other spouse. It is usually scheduled and requires some thought to execute, so the simplest way to overcome this Love Buster is to take it off your schedule. If your Thursday night bowling bothers your spouse, schedule something else Thursday night that your spouse would agree to enthusiastically.

One Love Buster we discussed, annoying habits, can be very difficult to overcome because they are repeated without much thought—even if you agree to avoid them, they seem come back out of nowhere. But independent behavior requires a deliberate decision every time you do it. Whenever you engage in independent behavior, you are aware of what you are doing.

If you follow the Policy of Joint Agreement (never do anything without an enthusiastic agreement between you and your spouse), you will never engage in independent behavior—any event or activity that is not mutually agreed to cannot take place. It forces you to take your spouse's interests and feelings into account when you forget that your spouse is an extremely important part of yourself, and should be considered in every decision you make.

Independent behavior is a problem in most marriages because we are all tempted to do whatever makes us happy, even when it makes our spouse unhappy. We don't feel the pain our spouse feels when we are inconsiderate—all we feel is the pleasure gained from activities that are in our best interest. That's why the Policy of Joint Agreement is so important in marriage. It forces us to behave as if we feel each other's pain—it makes us behave as if we were empathetic.

The wise alternative to independent behavior is interdependent behavior, which limits your events or activities to those you both enjoy. You are both happy and neither of you suffers when you make decisions with each other's feelings in mind.

The first step in eliminating independent behavior is for you to identify instances of it. The **Independent Behavior Inventory: Part 1** helps identify existing independent behavior that should be changed to interdependent behavior. List all the behaviors and activities of your spouse that are not carried out with your interests in mind. Every item listed represents a weakness in your marital lifestyle—a weakness that can destroy the love you have for your spouse. A simple decision to end each independent behavior listed is the easiest way to stop these Love Busters in their tracks.

But if you do not think you can stop the behavior so easily, complete the **Independent Behavior Inventory: Part 2** to create an understanding of why the behavior is so compelling. When independent behavior has become an addiction, you may find that there are serious emotional consequences when separated from the source of addiction. Whether it's bowling on Thursday night or having an affair, the independent behavior gives a spouse such intense pleasure that trying to eliminate it often leads to severe emotional symptoms of withdrawal—anxiety, depression, and anger. In spite of the suffering one spouse's independent behavior can cause the other, the pain of withdrawal is a serious obstacle to sweeping these Love Busters out of marriage.

If Part 2 indicates that addiction is at the root of the independent behavior, a treatment program for addicts may be your best strategy. First, try to overcome the behavior "cold turkey." But if you find yourself failing to resist temptation, enter a treatment program that guarantees separation from the source of addiction and provides support as you go through withdrawal. After the symptoms of withdrawal eventually subside, you will find yourself better able to avoid the independent behavior on your own.

But don't just eliminate independent behavior—create interdependent behavior to take its place. I have no objection to enjoyment to the point of addiction as long as your spouse is enjoying it with you. So in chapter 8 of *Love Busters*, I suggest Four Guidelines to Successful Negotiation to help you discover appropriate interdependent behavior.

The first guideline is to set ground rules for your discussion. Your conversation must be pleasant and safe. If either of you begin making demands, showing disrespect, or getting angry, break it off for another time. But if you find that you are rarely able to discuss a conflict with these ground rules in place, you should practice with issues of no consequence, just to get you into good negotiating habits. Negotiation can be fun, and if you approach it with a smile on your face, you will not only be more successful, but you will also negotiate more often.

The second guideline is to introduce the conflict and try to understand each other's perspectives. In this case, your conflict is finding an alternative behavior to take the place of the independent behavior you are eliminating. The information in **Independent Behavior Inventory: Part 2** can help you understand what motivates one of you to engage in the independent behavior. The **Independent Behavior Inventory: Part 3** gives the offended spouse the opportunity to explain why and how the independent behavior was unacceptable. From these two inventories, you provide information that can lead to the discovery of an alternative activity that gives the offending spouse what he or she needs, without causing the offended spouse to be unhappy.

The third guideline is to brainstorm. With the information in Parts 2 and 3, get your brains in gear and think of mutually agreeable alternatives to the independent behavior on the **Interdependent Behavior Possibilities Inventory**. Remember that your goal is to find a behavior or activity that addresses the reasons that the independent behavior existed, yet changes it to accommodate the feelings and interests of the other spouse as well. You should both carry a copy of this inventory with you throughout the day so that when you think of a possible solution, you can write it down.

The fourth guideline to successful negotiation is to find the solution that meets with your enthusiastic agreement. Each day you should look over each other's lists to see if a mutually acceptable solution has been found. When you think you have found it, try it out for a while to see if it works as well as you had hoped. If you are both happy with your decision, your negotiation has ended successfully.

Note: You may need multiple copies of these forms, so be sure to photocopy them rather than writing in the book.

Independent Behavior Inventory: Part 1

* This questionnaire is to be completed by the spouse bothered by the behavior

Independent behavior is the conduct of one spouse that ignores the feelings and interests of the other spouse. It is usually scheduled and requires some thought to execute. Such behavior may include sporting events you attend, your choice of church, or your personal exercise program.

Please list your spouse's independent behaviors. (1) Name the behavior, (2) describe it, (3) indicate the frequency with which it occurs, and (4) use a number from 0 to 10 to indicate the intensity at which it bothers you (0 = not at all, 10 = extremely).

1. Name of behavior: _____

   Description of behavior: _____

   _____

   Frequency: _____ Intensity: _____

2. Name of behavior: _____

   Description of behavior: _____

   _____

   Frequency: _____ Intensity: _____

3. Name of behavior: _____

   Description of behavior: _____

   _____

   Frequency: _____ Intensity: _____

4. Name of behavior: _____

   Description of behavior: _____

   _____

   Frequency: _____ Intensity: _____

5. Name of behavior: _____

   Description of behavior: _____

   _____

   Frequency: _____ Intensity: _____

Independent Behavior Inventory: Part 2

* This questionnaire is to be completed by the spouse with the independent behavior

• •

All of the following questions apply to this independent behavior:_____

_____

• •

1. When did you begin to engage in this behavior?

   _____

   _____

2. What are the most important reasons you began to engage in this behavior?

   _____

   _____

3. What are the most important reasons you engage in this behavior now?

   _____

   _____

4. When you engage in this behavior, how do you feel?

   _____

5. When you engage in this behavior, how does your spouse feel?

   _____

6. Have you ever tried to avoid this behavior?_____ If so, how did you do it?

   _____

   _____

7. If you decided to avoid this behavior entirely, would you be successful?_____
   Why or why not?

   _____

   _____

8. Are you willing to avoid this behavior?_____

9. If you have any suggestions that would make elimination of this behavior more likely,
   please write them on a separate sheet of paper and attach it to this form.

Independent Behavior Inventory: Part 3

* This questionnaire is to be completed by the spouse bothered by the independent behavior

• •

All of the following questions apply to this independent behavior:_____

_____

• •

1. What bothers you about this independent behavior?

_____

_____

_____

_____

_____

_____

2. What doesn't bother you about this independent behavior?

_____

_____

_____

_____

_____

_____

3. Your spouse engages in this behavior because it is enjoyable to him/her. How might the behavior be changed so that it is enjoyable for both of you?

_____

_____

_____

_____

_____

_____

_____

_____

Interdependent Behavior Possibilities Inventory

* This questionnaire is to be completed by both spouses together

This inventory applies to the following independent behavior:_____

_____

   Please name and describe activities that might replace the independent behavior. Keep adding activities to this list until you find one that meets with your mutual enthusiastic agreement. Your goal is to find a behavior or activity that addresses the reasons that the independent behavior existed, yet changes it to accommodate the feelings and interests of the other spouse as well. You should both carry a copy of this inventory with you throughout the day so that when you think of a possible solution, you can write it down.

_____

_____

_____

_____

_____

_____

_____

_____

_____

_____

_____

_____

_____

_____

_____

_____

_____

_____

_____

_____

_____

_____

_____

_____

_____

Identifying the Most Important Emotional Needs

When your most important emotional needs are met by your spouse, he/she deposits the greatest possible number of love units into your Love Bank, and you experience romantic love toward your spouse. The same is true for your spouse. When you meet his/her most important emotional needs, he/she experiences romantic love for you (as long as Love Busters don't withdraw all the love units you deposit).

You're the only one who can identify your most important emotional needs. Only you know what your spouse can do to give you the best feelings possible. So I've designed forms to help you communicate your needs to your spouse and to help your spouse communicate his/her needs to you.

The **His Emotional Needs Questionnaire** helps the husband identify his most important emotional needs, and the **Her Emotional Needs Questionnaire** helps the wife identify her most important emotional needs. When you have both completed these questionnaires, you will have identified for each other your five most important emotional needs, and you will have ranked them according to the pleasure each of you receives when these needs are met. The needs rated highest give you the most pleasure and deposit the most love units when they are met.

Both of these questionnaires are printed in the back of *His Needs, Her Needs*.* In this workbook you'll have space to describe your feelings about these needs.

* In early printings the form was called "Analysis of His [Her] Marital Needs Questionnaire."

In order to understand these needs better, you may want to familiarize yourself with them by reading chapters 3–12 of *His Needs, Her Needs*.

If you can learn to meet your spouse's five most important emotional needs, and your spouse can learn to meet yours, you'll find each other irresistible! To discover these important emotional needs, complete these two questionnaires.

Her Emotional Needs Questionnaire

This questionnaire is designed to help you determine your most important emotional needs and evaluate your spouse's effectiveness in meeting those needs. Answer all the questions as candidly as possible. Do not try to minimize any needs that you feel have been unmet. If your answers require more space, use and attach a separate sheet of paper.

Your spouse should complete an **Emotional Needs Questionnaire** so that you can discover his needs and evaluate your effectiveness in meeting those needs.

When you have completed this questionnaire, go through it a second time to be certain your answers accurately reflect your feelings. Do not erase your original answers, but cross them out lightly so that your husband can see the corrections and discuss them with you.

The final page of this questionnaire asks you to identify and rank five of the ten needs in order of their importance to you. The most important emotional needs are those that give you the most pleasure when met and frustrate you the most when unmet. Resist the temptation to identify as most important only those needs that your spouse is not presently meeting. Include *all* your emotional needs in your consideration of those that are most important.

1. **Affection:** Showing love through words, cards, gifts, hugs, kisses, and courtesies; creating an environment that clearly and repeatedly expresses love.

   A. **Need for affection:** Indicate how much you need affection by circling the appropriate number.

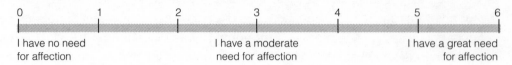

   | 0 | 1 | 2 | 3 | 4 | 5 | 6 |

   I have no need   I have a moderate   I have a great need
   for affection   need for affection   for affection

   • If or when your spouse is not affectionate with you, how do you feel? (Circle the appropriate letter.)

     a. Very unhappy   c. Neither happy nor unhappy

     b. Somewhat unhappy   d. Happy not to be shown affection

   • If or when your spouse is affectionate to you, how do you feel? (Circle the appropriate letter.)

     a. Very happy   c. Neither happy nor unhappy

     b. Somewhat happy   d. Unhappy to be shown affection

   B. **Evaluation of spouse's affection:** Indicate your satisfaction with your spouse's affection toward you by circling the appropriate number.

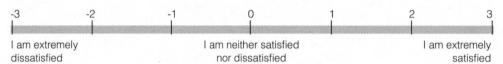

   | -3 | -2 | -1 | 0 | 1 | 2 | 3 |

   I am extremely   I am neither satisfied   I am extremely
   dissatisfied   nor dissatisfied   satisfied

   • My spouse gives me all the affection I need.   Yes   No

     If your answer is no, how often would you like your spouse to be affectionate with you?

     _____ times each day/week/month.
     (write number)   (circle one)

   • I like the way my spouse gives me affection.   Yes   No

     If your answer is no, explain how your need for affection could be better satisfied in your marriage.

     _____

     _____

     _____

2. **Sexual Fulfillment:** A sexual relationship that brings out a predictably enjoyable sexual response in both of you that is frequent enough for both of you.

A. **Need for sexual fulfillment:** Indicate how much you need sexual fulfillment by circling the appropriate number.

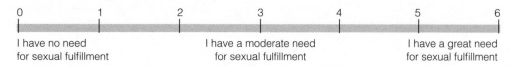

| 0 | 1 | 2 | 3 | 4 | 5 | 6 |

I have no need
for sexual fulfillment

I have a moderate need
for sexual fulfillment

I have a great need
for sexual fulfillment

- If or when your spouse is not willing to engage in sexual relations with you, how do you feel? (Circle the appropriate letter.)

    a. Very unhappy   c. Neither happy nor unhappy

    b. Somewhat unhappy   d. Happy not to engage in sexual relations

- If or when your spouse engages in sexual relations with you, how do you feel? (Circle the appropriate letter.)

    a. Very happy   c. Neither happy nor unhappy

    b. Somewhat happy   d. Unhappy to engage in sexual relations

B. **Evaluation of sexual relations with your spouse:** Indicate your satisfaction with your spouse's sexual relations with you by circling the appropriate number.

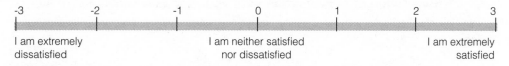

| -3 | -2 | -1 | 0 | 1 | 2 | 3 |

I am extremely
dissatisfied

I am neither satisfied
nor dissatisfied

I am extremely
satisfied

- My spouse has sexual relations with me as often as I need. Yes   No

    If your answer is no, how often would you like your spouse to have sex with you?

    _____ times each day/week/month.

    (write number)   (circle one)

- I like the way my spouse has sexual relations with me. Yes   No

    If your answer is no, explain how your need for sexual fulfillment could be better satisfied in your marriage.

    _____

    _____

    _____

3. **Conversation:** Talking about events of the day, feelings, and plans; avoiding angry or judgmental statements or dwelling on past mistakes; showing interest in your favorite topics of conversation; balancing conversation; using it to inform, investigate, and understand you; and giving you undivided attention.

A. **Need for conversation:** Indicate how much you need conversation by circling the appropriate number.

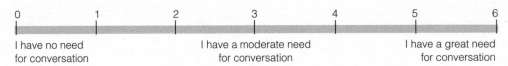

- If or when your spouse is not willing to talk with you, how do you feel? (Circle the appropriate letter.)

  a. Very unhappy   c. Neither happy nor unhappy

  b. Somewhat unhappy   d. Happy not to talk

- If or when your spouse talks to you, how do you feel? (Circle the appropriate letter.)

  a. Very happy   c. Neither happy nor unhappy

  b. Somewhat happy   d. Unhappy to talk

B. **Evaluation of conversation with your spouse:** Indicate your satisfaction with your spouse's conversation with you by circling the appropriate number.

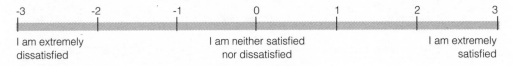

- My spouse talks to me as often as I need.   Yes   No

  If your answer is no, how often would you like your spouse to talk to you?

  _____ times each day/week/month.

  (write number)   (circle one)

- I like the way my spouse talks to me.   Yes   No

  If your answer is no, explain how your need for conversation could be better satisfied in your marriage.

  _____

  _____

  _____

4. **Recreational Companionship:** Developing interest in your favorite recreational activities, learning to be proficient in them, and joining you in those activities. If any prove to be unpleasant to your spouse after an effort has been made, negotiating new activities that are mutually enjoyable.

A. **Need for recreational companionship:** Indicate how much you need recreational companionship by circling the appropriate number.

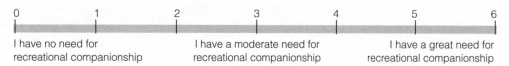

| 0 | 1 | 2 | 3 | 4 | 5 | 6 |

I have no need for recreational companionship

I have a moderate need for recreational companionship

I have a great need for recreational companionship

- If or when your spouse is not willing to join you in recreational activities, how do you feel? (Circle the appropriate letter.)

    a. Very unhappy
    b. Somewhat unhappy
    c. Neither happy nor unhappy
    d. Happy not to include my spouse

- If or when your spouse joins you in recreational activities, how do you feel? (Circle the appropriate letter.)

    a. Very happy
    b. Somewhat happy
    c. Neither happy nor unhappy
    d. Unhappy to join in recreational activities

B. **Evaluation of recreational companionship with your spouse:** Indicate your satisfaction with your spouse's recreational companionship by circling the appropriate number.

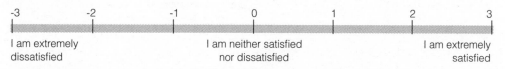

| -3 | -2 | -1 | 0 | 1 | 2 | 3 |

I am extremely dissatisfied

I am neither satisfied nor dissatisfied

I am extremely satisfied

- My spouse joins me in recreational activities as often as I need.   Yes   No

    If your answer is no, how often would you like your spouse to join you in recreational activities?

    _____ times each day/week/month.
    (write number)   (circle one)

- I like the way my spouse joins me in recreational activities.   Yes   No

    If your answer is no, explain how your need for recreational companionship could be better satisfied in your marriage.

    _____

    _____

    _____

5. **Honesty and Openness:** Revealing positive and negative feelings, events of the past, daily events and schedule, plans for the future; not leaving you with a false impression; answering your questions truthfully.

A. **Need for honesty and openness:** Indicate how much you need honesty and openness by circling the appropriate number.

I have no need
for honesty and openness

I have a moderate need
for honesty and openness

I have a great need
for honesty and openness

- If or when your spouse is not open and honest with you, how do you feel? (Circle the appropriate letter.)

    a. Very unhappy   c. Neither happy nor unhappy

    b. Somewhat unhappy   d. Happy not to be honest and open

- If or when your spouse is open and honest with you, how do you feel? (Circle the appropriate letter.)

    a. Very happy   c. Neither happy nor unhappy

    b. Somewhat happy   d. Unhappy to be honest and open

B. **Evaluation of spouse's honesty and openness:** Indicate your satisfaction with your spouse's honesty and openness by circling the appropriate number.

I am extremely
dissatisfied

I am neither satisfied
nor dissatisfied

I am extremely
satisfied

- In which of the following areas of honesty and openness would you like to see improvement from your spouse? (Circle the letters that apply to you.)

    a. Sharing positive and negative emotional reactions to significant aspects of life

    b. Sharing information regarding his personal history

    c. Sharing information about his daily activities

    d. Sharing information about his future schedule and plans

If you circled any of the above, explain how your need for honesty and openness could be better satisfied in your marriage.

_____

_____

_____

6. **Attractiveness of Spouse:** Keeping physically fit with diet and exercise; wearing hair and clothing in a way that you find attractive and tasteful.

   A. **Need for an attractive spouse:** Indicate how much you need an attractive spouse by circling the appropriate number.

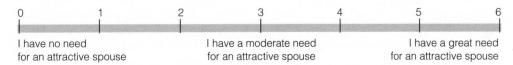

   - If or when your spouse is not willing to make the most of his physical attractiveness, how do you feel? (Circle the appropriate letter.)

     a. Very unhappy   c. Neither happy nor unhappy

     b. Somewhat unhappy   d. Happy he does not make an effort

   - When your spouse makes the most of his physical attractiveness, how do you feel? (Circle the appropriate letter.)

     a. Very happy   c. Neither happy nor unhappy

     b. Somewhat happy   d. Unhappy to see him make an effort

   B. **Evaluation of spouse's attractiveness:** Indicate your satisfaction with your spouse's attractiveness by circling the appropriate number.

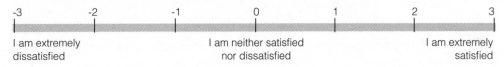

   - In which of the following characteristics of attractiveness would you like to see improvement from your spouse? (Circle the letters that apply.)

     a. Physical fitness and normal weight

     b. Attractive choice of clothes

     c. Attractive hairstyle

     d. Good physical hygiene

     e. Other _____

   If you circled any of the above, explain how your need for an attractive spouse could be better satisfied in your marriage.

   _____

   _____

   _____

7. **Financial Support:** Provision of the financial resources to house, feed, and clothe your family at a standard of living acceptable to you, but avoiding travel and working hours that are unacceptable to you.

    A. **Need for financial support:** Indicate how much you need financial support by circling the appropriate number.

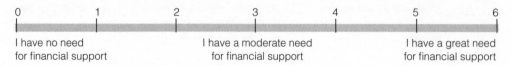

| 0 | 1 | 2 | 3 | 4 | 5 | 6 |

I have no need
for financial support

I have a moderate need
for financial support

I have a great need
for financial support

- If or when your spouse is not willing to support you financially, how do you feel? (Circle the appropriate letter.)

    a. Very unhappy   c. Neither happy nor unhappy

    b. Somewhat unhappy   d. Happy not to be financially supported

- If or when your spouse supports you financially, how do you feel? (Circle the appropriate letter.)

    a. Very happy   c. Neither happy nor unhappy

    b. Somewhat happy   d. Unhappy to be financially supported

    B. **Evaluation of spouse's financial support:** Indicate your satisfaction with your spouse's financial support by circling the appropriate number.

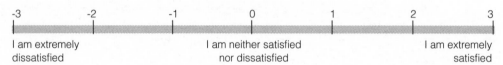

| -3 | -2 | -1 | 0 | 1 | 2 | 3 |

I am extremely
dissatisfied

I am neither satisfied
nor dissatisfied

I am extremely
satisfied

- How much money would you like your spouse to earn to support you?

- How many hours each week would you like your spouse to work?

If your spouse is not earning as much as you would like, is not working the hours you would like, does not budget the way you would like, or does not earn an income the way you would like, explain how your need for financial support could be better satisfied in your marriage.

_____

_____

_____

_____

8. **Domestic Support:** Creation of a home environment for you that offers a refuge from the stresses of life; managing the home and care of the children—if any are at home—including but not limited to cooking meals, washing dishes, washing and ironing clothes, housecleaning.

A. **Need for domestic support:** Indicate how much you need domestic support by circling the appropriate number.

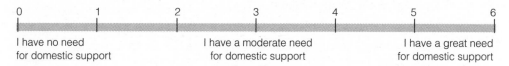

| 0 | 1 | 2 | 3 | 4 | 5 | 6 |

I have no need
for domestic support

I have a moderate need
for domestic support

I have a great need
for domestic support

- If your spouse is not willing to provide you with domestic support, how do you feel? (Circle the appropriate letter.)

    a. Very unhappy   c. Neither happy nor unhappy

    b. Somewhat unhappy   d. Happy not to have domestic support

- If or when your spouse provides you with domestic support, how do you feel? (Circle the appropriate letter.)

    a. Very happy   c. Neither happy nor unhappy

    b. Somewhat happy   d. Unhappy to have domestic support

B. **Evaluation of spouse's domestic support:** Indicate your satisfaction with your spouse's domestic support by circling the appropriate number.

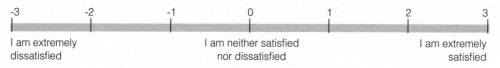

| -3 | -2 | -1 | 0 | 1 | 2 | 3 |

I am extremely
dissatisfied

I am neither satisfied
nor dissatisfied

I am extremely
satisfied

- My spouse provides me with all the domestic support I need.   Yes   No

- I like the way my spouse provides domestic support.   Yes   No

If your answer is no to either of the above questions, explain how your need for domestic support could be better satisfied in your marriage.

_____

_____

_____

_____

_____

9. **Family Commitment:** Scheduling sufficient time and energy for the moral and educational development of your children; reading to them, taking them on frequent outings, educating himself in appropriate child-training methods and discussing those methods with you; avoiding any child-training method or disciplinary action that does not have your enthusiastic support.

A. **Need for family commitment:** Indicate how much you need family commitment by circling the appropriate number.

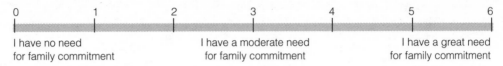

| 0 | 1 | 2 | 3 | 4 | 5 | 6 |

I have no need
for family commitment

I have a moderate need
for family commitment

I have a great need
for family commitment

- If or when your spouse is not willing to provide family commitment, how do you feel? (Circle the appropriate letter.)

    a. Very unhappy   c. Neither happy nor unhappy

    b. Somewhat unhappy   d. Happy he's not involved

- If or when your spouse provides family commitment, how do you feel? (Circle the appropriate letter.)

    a. Very happy   c. Neither happy nor unhappy

    b. Somewhat happy   d. Unhappy he's involved in the family

B. **Evaluation of spouse's family commitment:** Indicate your satisfaction with your spouse's family commitment by circling the appropriate number.

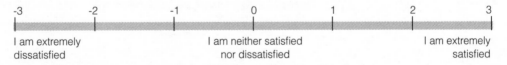

| -3 | -2 | -1 | 0 | 1 | 2 | 3 |

I am extremely
dissatisfied

I am neither satisfied
nor dissatisfied

I am extremely
satisfied

- My spouse commits enough time to the family.   Yes   No

    If your answer is no, how often would you like your spouse to join in family activities?

    _____ times each day/week/month.

    (write number)   (circle one)

- I like the way my spouse spends time with the family.   Yes   No

    If your answer is no, explain how your need for family commitment could be better satisfied in your marriage.

    _____

    _____

    _____

10. **Admiration:** Respecting, valuing, and appreciating you; rarely critical and expressing admiration to you clearly and often.

A. **Need for admiration:** Indicate how much you need admiration by circling the appropriate number.

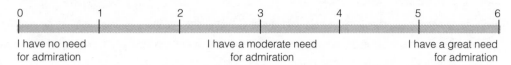

0	1	2	3	4	5	6

I have no need
for admiration

I have a moderate need
for admiration

I have a great need
for admiration

- If or when your spouse does not admire you, how do you feel? (Circle the appropriate letter.)

    a. Very unhappy   c. Neither happy nor unhappy

    b. Somewhat unhappy   d. Happy not to be admired

- If or when your spouse does admire you, how do you feel? (Circle the appropriate letter.)

    a. Very happy   c. Neither happy nor unhappy

    b. Somewhat happy   d. Unhappy to be admired

B. **Evaluation of spouse's admiration:** Indicate your satisfaction with your spouse's admiration of you by circling the appropriate number.

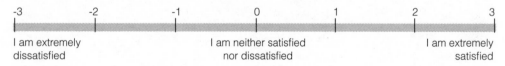

-3	-2	-1	0	1	2	3

I am extremely
dissatisfied

I am neither satisfied
nor dissatisfied

I am extremely
satisfied

- My spouse gives me all the admiration I need.   Yes   No

    If your answer is no, how often would you like your spouse to admire you?

    _____ times each day/week/month.

    (write number)   (circle one)

- I like the way my spouse admires me.   Yes   No

    If your answer is no, explain how your need for admiration could be better satisfied in your marriage.

    _____

    _____

    _____

    _____

    _____

Ranking Her Emotional Needs

The ten basic emotional needs are listed below. There is also space for you to add other emotional needs that you feel are essential to your marital happiness.

In the space provided in front of each need, write a number from 1 to 5 that ranks the need's importance to your happiness. Write a 1 before the most important need, a 2 before the next most important, and so on until you have ranked your five most important needs.

To help you rank these needs, imagine that you will have only one need met in your marriage. Which would make you the happiest, knowing that all the others would go unmet? That need should be 1. If only two needs will be met, what would your second selection be? Which five needs, when met, would make you the happiest?

_____ Affection

_____ Sexual fulfillment

_____ Conversation

_____ Recreational companionship

_____ Honesty and openness

_____ Attractiveness of spouse

_____ Financial support

_____ Domestic support

_____ Family commitment

_____ Admiration

_____ _____

_____ _____

_____ _____

_____ _____

His Emotional Needs Questionnaire

This questionnaire is designed to help you determine your most important emotional needs and evaluate your spouse's effectiveness in meeting those needs. Answer all the questions as candidly as possible. Do not try to minimize any needs that you feel have been unmet. If your answers require more space, use and attach a separate sheet of paper.

Your spouse should complete an **Emotional Needs Questionnaire** so that you can discover her needs and evaluate your effectiveness in meeting those needs.

When you have completed this questionnaire, go through it a second time to be certain your answers accurately reflect your feelings. Do not erase your original answers, but cross them out lightly so that your wife can see the corrections and discuss them with you.

The final page of this questionnaire asks you to identify and rank five of the ten needs in order of their importance to you. The most important emotional needs are those that give you the most pleasure when met and frustrate you the most when unmet. Resist the temptation to identify as most important only those needs that your spouse is not presently meeting. Include *all* your emotional needs in your consideration of those that are most important.

1. **Affection:** Showing love through words, cards, gifts, hugs, kisses, and courtesies; creating an environment that clearly and repeatedly expresses love.

   A. **Need for affection:** Indicate how much you need affection by circling the appropriate number.

   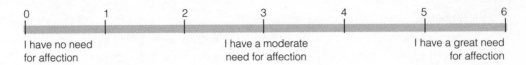

   I have no need   I have a moderate   I have a great need
   for affection   need for affection   for affection

   - If or when your spouse is not affectionate with you, how do you feel? (Circle the appropriate letter.)

     a. Very unhappy   c. Neither happy nor unhappy

     b. Somewhat unhappy   d. Happy not to be shown affection

   - If or when your spouse is affectionate to you, how do you feel? (Circle the appropriate letter.)

     a. Very happy   c. Neither happy nor unhappy

     b. Somewhat happy   d. Unhappy to be shown affection

   B. **Evaluation of spouse's affection:** Indicate your satisfaction with your spouse's affection toward you by circling the appropriate number.

   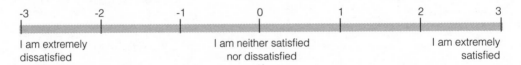

   I am extremely   I am neither satisfied   I am extremely
   dissatisfied   nor dissatisfied   satisfied

   - My spouse gives me all the affection I need.   Yes   No

     If your answer is no, how often would you like your spouse to be affectionate with you?

     _____ times each day/week/month.

     (write number)   (circle one)

   - I like the way my spouse gives me affection.   Yes   No

     If your answer is no, explain how your need for affection could be better satisfied in your marriage.

     _____

     _____

     _____

2. **Sexual Fulfillment:** A sexual relationship that brings out a predictably enjoyable sexual response in both of you that is frequent enough for both of you.

   A. **Need for sexual fulfillment:** Indicate how much you need sexual fulfillment by circling the appropriate number.

| 0 | 1 | 2 | 3 | 4 | 5 | 6 |

I have no need for sexual fulfillment   I have a moderate need for sexual fulfillment   I have a great need for sexual fulfillment

- If or when your spouse is not willing to engage in sexual relations with you, how do you feel? (Circle the appropriate letter.)

    a. Very unhappy   c. Neither happy nor unhappy

    b. Somewhat unhappy   d. Happy not to engage in sexual relations

- If or when your spouse engages in sexual relations with you, how do you feel? (Circle the appropriate letter.)

    a. Very happy   c. Neither happy nor unhappy

    b. Somewhat happy   d. Unhappy to engage in sexual relations

   B. **Evaluation of sexual relations with your spouse:** Indicate your satisfaction with your spouse's sexual relations with you by circling the appropriate number.

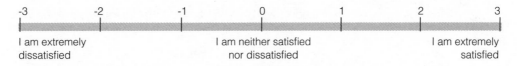

| -3 | -2 | -1 | 0 | 1 | 2 | 3 |

I am extremely dissatisfied   I am neither satisfied nor dissatisfied   I am extremely satisfied

- My spouse has sexual relations with me as often as I need.   Yes   No

If your answer is no, how often would you like your spouse to have sex with you?

_____ times each day/week/month.

(write number)   (circle one)

- I like the way my spouse has sexual relations with me.   Yes   No

If your answer is no, explain how your need for sexual fulfillment could be better satisfied in your marriage.

_____

_____

_____

3. **Conversation:** Talking about events of the day, feelings, and plans; avoiding angry or judgmental statements or dwelling on past mistakes; showing interest in your favorite topics of conversation; balancing conversation; using it to inform, investigate, and understand you; and giving you undivided attention.

A. **Need for conversation:** Indicate how much you need conversation by circling the appropriate number.

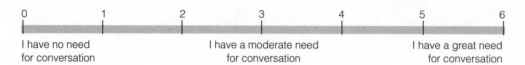

0   1   2   3   4   5   6

I have no need for conversation   I have a moderate need for conversation   I have a great need for conversation

- If or when your spouse is not willing to talk with you, how do you feel? (Circle the appropriate letter.)

  a. Very unhappy   c. Neither happy nor unhappy

  b. Somewhat unhappy   d. Happy not to talk

- If or when your spouse talks to you, how do you feel? (Circle the appropriate letter.)

  a. Very happy   c. Neither happy nor unhappy

  b. Somewhat happy   d. Unhappy to talk

B. **Evaluation of conversation with your spouse:** Indicate your satisfaction with your spouse's conversation with you by circling the appropriate number.

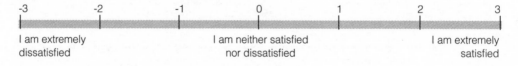

-3   -2   -1   0   1   2   3

I am extremely dissatisfied   I am neither satisfied nor dissatisfied   I am extremely satisfied

- My spouse talks to me as often as I need.   Yes   No

  If your answer is no, how often would you like your spouse to talk to you?

  _____ times each day/week/month.

  (write number)   (circle one)

- I like the way my spouse talks to me.   Yes   No

  If your answer is no, explain how your need for conversation could be better satisfied in your marriage.

  _____

  _____

  _____

4. **Recreational Companionship:** Developing interest in your favorite recreational activities, learning to be proficient in them, and joining you in those activities. If any prove to be unpleasant to your spouse after an effort has been made, negotiating new activities that are mutually enjoyable.

   A. **Need for recreational companionship:** Indicate how much you need recreational companionship by circling the appropriate number.

   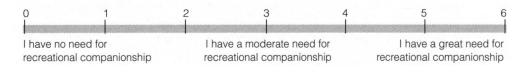

   | 0 | 1 | 2 | 3 | 4 | 5 | 6 |

   I have no need for recreational companionship   I have a moderate need for recreational companionship   I have a great need for recreational companionship

   - If or when your spouse is not willing to join you in recreational activities, how do you feel? (Circle the appropriate letter.)

     a. Very unhappy

     b. Somewhat unhappy

     c. Neither happy nor unhappy

     d. Happy not to include my spouse

   - If or when your spouse joins you in recreational activities, how do you feel? (Circle the appropriate letter.)

     a. Very happy

     b. Somewhat happy

     c. Neither happy nor unhappy

     d. Unhappy to join in recreational activities

   B. **Evaluation of recreational companionship with your spouse:** Indicate your satisfaction with your spouse's recreational companionship by circling the appropriate number.

   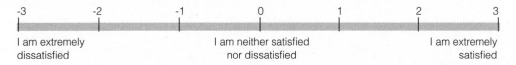

   | -3 | -2 | -1 | 0 | 1 | 2 | 3 |

   I am extremely dissatisfied   I am neither satisfied nor dissatisfied   I am extremely satisfied

   - My spouse joins me in recreational activities as often as I need.   Yes   No

     If your answer is no, how often would you like your spouse to join you in recreational activities?

     _____ times each day/week/month.

     (write number)   (circle one)

   - I like the way my spouse joins me in recreational activities.   Yes   No

     If your answer is no, explain how your need for recreational companionship could be better satisfied in your marriage.

     _____

     _____

     _____

5. **Honesty and Openness:** Revealing positive and negative feelings, events of the past, daily events and schedule, plans for the future; not leaving you with a false impression; answering your questions truthfully.

A. **Need for honesty and openness:** Indicate how much you need honesty and openness by circling the appropriate number.

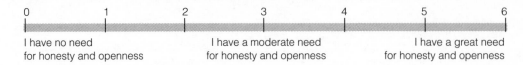

0   1   2   3   4   5   6

I have no need
for honesty and openness

I have a moderate need
for honesty and openness

I have a great need
for honesty and openness

- If or when your spouse is not open and honest with you, how do you feel? (Circle the appropriate letter.)

  a. Very unhappy   c. Neither happy nor unhappy

  b. Somewhat unhappy   d. Happy not to be honest and open

- If or when your spouse is open and honest with you, how do you feel? (Circle the appropriate letter.)

  a. Very happy   c. Neither happy nor unhappy

  b. Somewhat happy   d. Unhappy to be honest and open

B. **Evaluation of spouse's honesty and openness:** Indicate your satisfaction with your spouse's honesty and openness by circling the appropriate number.

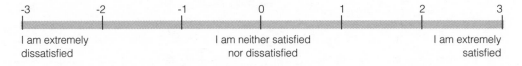

-3   -2   -1   0   1   2   3

I am extremely
dissatisfied

I am neither satisfied
nor dissatisfied

I am extremely
satisfied

- In which of the following areas of honesty and openness would you like to see improvement from your spouse? (Circle the letters that apply to you.)

  a. Sharing positive and negative emotional reactions to significant aspects of life

  b. Sharing information regarding her personal history

  c. Sharing information about her daily activities

  d. Sharing information about her future schedule and plans

If you circled any of the above, explain how your need for honesty and openness could be better satisfied in your marriage.

_____

_____

_____

6. **Attractiveness of Spouse:** Keeping physically fit with diet and exercise; wearing hair, clothing, and makeup in a way that you find attractive and tasteful.

A. **Need for an attractive spouse:** Indicate how much you need an attractive spouse by circling the appropriate number.

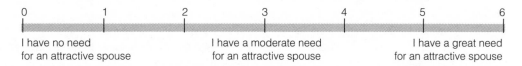

- If or when your spouse is not willing to make the most of her physical attractiveness, how do you feel? (Circle the appropriate letter.)

    a. Very unhappy
    c. Neither happy nor unhappy

    b. Somewhat unhappy
    d. Happy she does not make an effort

- When your spouse makes the most of her physical attractiveness, how do you feel? (Circle the appropriate letter.)

    a. Very happy
    c. Neither happy nor unhappy

    b. Somewhat happy
    d. Unhappy to see her make an effort

B. **Evaluation of spouse's attractiveness:** Indicate your satisfaction with your spouse's attractiveness by circling the appropriate number.

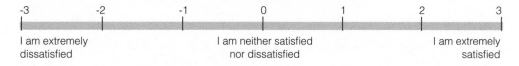

- In which of the following characteristics of attractiveness would you like to see improvement from your spouse? (Circle the letters that apply.)

    a. Physical fitness and normal weight

    b. Attractive choice of clothes

    c. Attractive hairstyle

    d. Good physical hygiene

    e. Attractive facial makeup

    f. Other _____

If you circled any of the above, explain how your need for an attractive spouse could be better satisfied in your marriage.

_____

_____

_____

7. **Financial Support:** Provision of the financial resources to house, feed, and clothe your family at a standard of living acceptable to you, but avoiding travel and working hours that are unacceptable to you.

A. **Need for financial support:** Indicate how much you need financial support by circling the appropriate number.

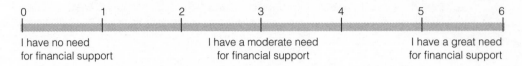

| 0 | 1 | 2 | 3 | 4 | 5 | 6 |

I have no need
for financial support

I have a moderate need
for financial support

I have a great need
for financial support

- If or when your spouse is not willing to support you financially, how do you feel? (Circle the appropriate letter.)

   a. Very unhappy   c. Neither happy nor unhappy

   b. Somewhat unhappy   d. Happy not to be financially supported

- If or when your spouse supports you financially, how do you feel? (Circle the appropriate letter.)

   a. Very happy   c. Neither happy nor unhappy

   b. Somewhat happy   d. Unhappy to be financially supported

B. **Evaluation of spouse's financial support:** Indicate your satisfaction with your spouse's financial support by circling the appropriate number.

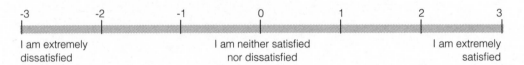

| -3 | -2 | -1 | 0 | 1 | 2 | 3 |

I am extremely
dissatisfied

I am neither satisfied
nor dissatisfied

I am extremely
satisfied

- How much money would you like your spouse to earn to support you?

- How many hours each week would you like your spouse to work?

   If your spouse is not earning as much as you would like, is not working the hours you would like, does not budget the way you would like, or does not earn an income the way you would like, explain how your need for financial support could be better satisfied in your marriage.

   _____

   _____

   _____

   _____

8. **Domestic Support:** Creation of a home environment for you that offers a refuge from the stresses of life; managing the home and care of the children—if any are at home—including but not limited to cooking meals, washing dishes, washing and ironing clothes, housecleaning.

A. **Need for domestic support:** Indicate how much you need domestic support by circling the appropriate number.

| 0 | 1 | 2 | 3 | 4 | 5 | 6 |

I have no need
for domestic support

I have a moderate need
for domestic support

I have a great need
for domestic support

- If your spouse is not willing to provide you with domestic support, how do you feel? (Circle the appropriate letter.)

    a. Very unhappy   c. Neither happy nor unhappy

    b. Somewhat unhappy   d. Happy not to have domestic support

- If or when your spouse provides you with domestic support, how do you feel? (Circle the appropriate letter.)

    a. Very happy   c. Neither happy nor unhappy

    b. Somewhat happy   d. Unhappy to have domestic support

B. **Evaluation of spouse's domestic support:** Indicate your satisfaction with your spouse's domestic support by circling the appropriate number.

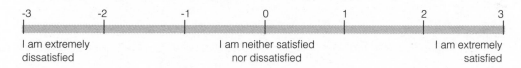

| -3 | -2 | -1 | 0 | 1 | 2 | 3 |

I am extremely
dissatisfied

I am neither satisfied
nor dissatisfied

I am extremely
satisfied

- My spouse provides me with all the domestic support I need.   Yes   No

- I like the way my spouse provides domestic support.   Yes   No

    If your answer is no to either of the above questions, explain how your need for domestic support could be better satisfied in your marriage.

    _____

    _____

    _____

    _____

9. **Family Commitment:** Scheduling sufficient time and energy for the moral and educational development of your children; reading to them, taking them on frequent outings, educating herself in appropriate child-training methods and discussing those methods with you; avoiding any child-training method or disciplinary action that does not have your enthusiastic support.

A. **Need for family commitment:** Indicate how much you need family commitment by circling the appropriate number.

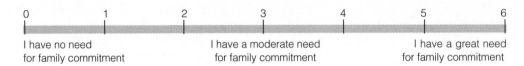

| 0 | 1 | 2 | 3 | 4 | 5 | 6 |

I have no need
for family commitment

I have a moderate need
for family commitment

I have a great need
for family commitment

- If or when your spouse is not willing to provide family commitment, how do you feel? (Circle the appropriate letter.)

    a. Very unhappy   c. Neither happy nor unhappy

    b. Somewhat unhappy   d. Happy she's not involved

- If or when your spouse provides family commitment, how do you feel? (Circle the appropriate letter.)

    a. Very happy   c. Neither happy nor unhappy

    b. Somewhat happy   d. Unhappy she's involved in the family

B. **Evaluation of spouse's family commitment:** Indicate your satisfaction with your spouse's family commitment by circling the appropriate number.

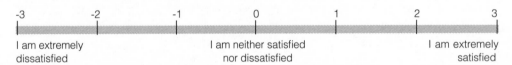

| -3 | -2 | -1 | 0 | 1 | 2 | 3 |

I am extremely
dissatisfied

I am neither satisfied
nor dissatisfied

I am extremely
satisfied

- My spouse commits enough time to the family.   Yes   No

    If your answer is no, how often would you like your spouse to join in family activities?

    _____ times each day/week/month.

    (write number)   (circle one)

- I like the way my spouse spends time with the family.   Yes   No

    If your answer is no, explain how your need for family commitment could be better satisfied in your marriage.

    _____

    _____

    _____

10. **Admiration:** Respecting, valuing, and appreciating you; rarely critical and expressing admiration to you clearly and often.

   A. **Need for admiration:** Indicate how much you need admiration by circling the appropriate number.

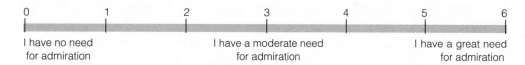

   - If or when your spouse does not admire you, how do you feel? (Circle the appropriate letter.)

     a. Very unhappy c. Neither happy nor unhappy

     b. Somewhat unhappy d. Happy not to be admired

   - If or when your spouse does admire you, how do you feel? (Circle the appropriate letter.)

     a. Very happy   c. Neither happy nor unhappy

     b. Somewhat happy d. Unhappy to be admired

   B. **Evaluation of spouse's admiration:** Indicate your satisfaction with your spouse's admiration of you by circling the appropriate number.

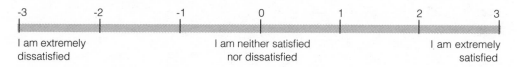

   - My spouse gives me all the admiration I need. Yes No

     If your answer is no, how often would you like your spouse to admire you?

     _____ times each day/week/month.
     (write number)   (circle one)

   - I like the way my spouse admires me. Yes No

     If your answer is no, explain how your need for admiration could be better satisfied in your marriage.

     _____

     _____

     _____

     _____

     _____

Ranking His Emotional Needs

The ten basic emotional needs are listed below. There is also space for you to add other emotional needs that you feel are essential to your marital happiness.

In the space provided in front of each need, write a number from 1 to 5 that ranks the need's importance to your happiness. Write a 1 before the most important need, a 2 before the next most important, and so on until you have ranked your five most important needs.

To help you rank these needs, imagine that you will have only one need met in your marriage. Which would make you the happiest, knowing that all the others would go unmet? That need should be 1. If only two needs will be met, what would your second selection be? Which five needs, when met, would make you the happiest?

_____ Affection

_____ Sexual fulfillment

_____ Conversation

_____ Recreational companionship

_____ Honesty and openness

_____ Attractiveness of spouse

_____ Financial support

_____ Domestic support

_____ Family commitment

_____ Admiration

_____ _____

_____ _____

_____ _____

_____ _____

Learning to Meet the Most Important Emotional Needs

We have finally reached the last step to romantic love. In this fifth step you will learn to deposit the most love units possible into your spouse's Love Bank. You will achieve this by meeting his/her most important emotional needs.

The reason I wait until the final step to teach you to meet each other's emotional needs is that you waste your effort if you've failed to overcome Love Busters (steps two and three) or failed to identify each other's emotional needs (step four). When you continue to cause your spouse emotional pain, your best effort to meet your spouse's needs is undone by your destructive habits. And when you don't know each other's emotional needs, your effort misses the mark.

If you've failed to eliminate Love Busters, your spouse may not let you meet his/her emotional needs. In order to be protected from the pain of Love Busters, your spouse may try to block out *all* emotional reactions to you, bad *and* good. So even if you're skilled in knowing how to meet emotional needs, your effort will be ineffective if you persist in Love Busters.

But when you eliminate your Love Busters, your spouse will drop the defenses and be willing to let you meet his/her emotional needs. It may be that you and your spouse already know how to meet each other's needs; in that case your romantic love is revived simply by overcoming Love Busters. If, however, after overcoming Love Busters, you find yourselves ineffective in meeting each other's needs, then you're ready to apply this final step to romantic love.

The results of the emotional needs questionnaires give you and your spouse a clear picture of each other's emotional needs and your effectiveness in meeting them. With these results you'll be able to put your effort where it will be appreciated the most. You're now ready to become skilled at meeting each other's five most important emotional needs. The chapters in *His Needs, Her Needs* are your guide to developing skill, and the forms in this workbook will help you organize and execute a plan to create that skill.

Learning to Meet the Need of Affection

Affection is *the* most important emotional need for many, if not most, women. While it is sometimes among the top five emotional needs of men, it is rarely at the top of the list. That's why it's so hard for some men to understand its critical importance to their wives.

In *His Needs, Her Needs*, chapter 3, I explain this tragic situation and how men can learn to become more affectionate. To illustrate my point, I describe a day in the life of an affectionate husband:

- He hugs and kisses his wife every morning while they are still in bed.
- He tells her that he loves her while they have breakfast together.
- He kisses her before leaving for work.
- He calls her during the day to see how she's doing.
- He buys her flowers once in a while as a surprise and includes his handwritten note expressing his love for her.
- After work, he calls her before he leaves for home, so that she can know when to expect him.
- When he arrives home from work, he gives her a hug and kiss and spends a few minutes talking to her about how her day went.
- He helps her with the dishes after dinner.
- He hugs and kisses her in bed before they go to sleep.

I've heard people complain that once affection becomes mechanical, or habitual, it loses its meaning. If it's not spontaneous, it doesn't reflect the deep feelings of affection. My answer to that complaint is that if you wait for spontaneity, you'll be waiting most of your lifetime, especially if your spouse doesn't share your intense need for affection.

Our behavior is not very spontaneous; it's essentially habitual. Most of what we do, we repeat again and again. We have limited information-processing capability, and our brains turn most of our behavior into habits so that we can devote our attention to emergencies and new situations. This is what makes our brains efficient. If we had to think about everything we did, we'd need brains the size of houses!

If your spouse needs affection, get used to the idea that you'll have to learn "habits" of affection. If they seem boring or mechanical to your spouse, the truth is that you've failed to develop habits that actually meet his/her need for affection. Learning to develop the correct habits of affection requires knowing something about your spouse's reaction to your affectionate habits.

I've designed a form to help you identify habits that meet your spouse's need for affection. The **Affection Inventory** not only helps you identify behavior that your spouse needs, but it also helps identify misguided behavior, affectionate behavior that is more annoying than fulfilling.

The inventory instructions suggest that since affection is interactive (one of you cannot be affectionate without the other participating), you and your spouse should complete separate inventories. After reviewing each other's tastes in affection, try to develop habits of affection that you both want to create, and try to avoid habits that either of you finds annoying.

Once you have identified affectionate habits that your spouse would like you to create and others that you should avoid, decide on a plan that will help you form desirable habits and avoid undesirable ones. To help you document the plan you intend to follow, I've included the **Strategy to Meet the Need of Affection** form.

When your plan is implemented, use the **Affection Worksheet** to document your progress. It's designed to give your spouse an opportunity to provide positive and negative feedback for your efforts. Instances of your affection are documented, along with your spouse's reaction to those instances. Sometimes negative feedback (your spouse lets you know that your effort did not meet his/her need for affection) can be a depressing moment. If you can rise above the momentary failure and redirect your effort, in the end you will learn to be affectionate in a way that meets your spouse's need for affection. Meeting that need will probably deposit more love units than meeting any other single need.

Note: You may need multiple copies of these forms, so be sure to photocopy them rather than writing in the book.

Affection Inventory

Under the heading Affectionate Habits to Create, please name and describe the types of affectionate behavior that you would like from your spouse. For example, if you would like your spouse to hold your hand more often, you should simply indicate how often and under which circumstances you would enjoy holding his/her hand.

If your spouse engages in affectionate behavior that you find annoying or inappropriate for your needs, name and describe that behavior under the heading Affectionate Habits to Avoid. You may find that it isn't the behavior itself that you consider inappropriate, but rather the time and place that bother you. If that's the case, explain that clearly in your description and include the appropriate circumstances under Affectionate Habits to Create. If you need more space for your descriptions or would like to list more habits than the form allows, use another sheet of paper and attach it to this form.

Since affection is interactive (one of you can't be affectionate without the other participating), you and your spouse should complete separate **Affection Inventories**. After reviewing each other's tastes in affection, try to develop habits of affection that you both want to create, and try to avoid habits that either of you finds annoying.

Affectionate Habits to Create

1. _____
_____
_____

2. _____
_____
_____

3. _____
_____
_____

4. _____
_____
_____
_____

5. _____

_____

_____

6. _____

_____

_____

Affectionate Habits to Avoid

1. _____

_____

_____

2. _____

_____

_____

3. _____

_____

_____

4. _____

_____

_____

5. _____

_____

_____

6. _____

_____

_____

Strategy to Meet the Need of Affection

· ·

This form is designed to help you create a strategy to meet your spouse's need for affection. Complete each section to provide yourself with documentation of the process you used to select a strategy.

· ·

1. Referring to your spouse's **Affection Inventory**, describe affectionate behavior that your spouse would like you to learn.

   _____

   _____

   _____

   _____

   _____

   _____

2. Describe your plan to learn the affectionate behavior listed in question 1. Be certain that this plan is made with the enthusiastic agreement of both you and your spouse. Include a deadline to learn this affectionate behavior.

   _____

   _____

   _____

   _____

   _____

   _____

3. If your plan does not succeed within your designated time limit, will you agree to seek professional help to learn affectionate behavior? How will you go about finding that help?

   _____

   _____

   _____

   _____

   _____

   _____

4. Describe the affectionate behavior that your spouse would like you to avoid.

_____

_____

_____

_____

_____

_____

5. Describe your plan to avoid the affectionate behavior listed in question 4. Be certain this plan is made with the enthusiastic agreement of both you and your spouse. Include a deadline to avoid this behavior.

_____

_____

_____

_____

_____

_____

6. If your plan to avoid unwanted affectionate behavior does not succeed within your designated time limit, will you agree to seek professional help to avoid this behavior? How will you go about finding that help?

_____

_____

_____

_____

_____

_____

Affection Worksheet

Please list all instances of your spouse's affection and your emotional reaction. If you find your spouse emotionally upset with your honest reactions, or if you are reluctant to provide honest reactions, seek professional supervision.

	Day	Date	Time	Type of Affection and Your Reaction
1.	_____	_____	_____	_____
2.	_____	_____	_____	_____
3.	_____	_____	_____	_____
4.	_____	_____	_____	_____
5.	_____	_____	_____	_____
6.	_____	_____	_____	_____
7.	_____	_____	_____	_____
8.	_____	_____	_____	_____

Learning to Meet the Need of Sexual Fulfillment

While affection is usually a woman's most important emotional need, sexual fulfillment is usually a man's most important emotional need. Some women will list sexual fulfillment among their top five emotional needs, but it's rarely number one. Almost all men include it among the top five, and most consider it to be first.

Women are usually aware of the importance of sex to men and make an effort to meet this need. But many fail to understand that simply having sex doesn't usually meet a man's need. Unless a woman joins her husband in the sexual experience, his need for sex goes unmet. One spouse cannot achieve sexual fulfillment in marriage unless the other spouse is also sexually fulfilled. So the strategy for achieving sexual fulfillment in a man often focuses on his wife's struggle to find sexual fulfillment.

Men and women differ dramatically in the way they come to enjoy sex. If these differences are not understood, or are ignored, a couple will find themselves sexually incompatible. As I explain in chapter 4 of *His Needs, Her Needs*, sexual compatibility is achieved when a couple overcomes sexual ignorance and communicates sexual understanding to each other. There's a third point that is also essential to sexual compatibility: A couple needs to accommodate each other's sexual preferences and reactions.

A husband and wife overcome sexual ignorance by each understanding their own sexual response. Women are often at a disadvantage since they usually come into marriage having experienced fewer sexual reactions than men. Men usually know what an orgasm is by adolescence, but some women go through life without having experienced one. Some women feel that sexual feelings are either disgusting or unnecessary because of the relative difficulty they have creating those feelings. But once a woman learns to respond sexually with little effort, her attitude toward sex usually changes dramatically.

The five stages of the sexual experience are (1) willingness, (2) arousal, (3) plateau, (4) climax, and (5) recovery (see chapter 4 of *His Needs, Her Needs*). Couples that experience these stages together when they make love usually consider themselves sexually compatible and usually tell me that they're sexually fulfilled. So if you want to achieve that outcome in your own sexual relationship, both you and your spouse should understand what these stages of the sexual experience are and learn how to experience them together.

I've designed the **Sexual Experience Inventory** to help you and your spouse determine your understanding of, and ability to experience, the five stages. When this inventory is completed, and stages of sexual experience have been identified as difficult for one or both of you, create a plan to overcome that difficulty. The **Strategy to Discover the Five Stages of Sexual Experience** is a form that will help you document your plan. After you have a plan, use the **Sexual Experience Worksheet** to document progress toward successful completion of your plan.

If you and your spouse know how to share the five stages of sexual experience when you make love, but have not found sexual fulfillment, there are probably Love Busters lurking in the background, preventing you from meeting each other's emotional needs. But in case that's not it, I've included forms that you can use to try to resolve your problem. *Do not use these forms until you have learned to experience the five stages when you make love.* The **Sexual Fulfillment Inventory** is designed to help you discover sexual habits that you or your spouse feel should either be created or avoided if your need is to be met. The **Strategy to Meet the Need of Sexual Fulfillment** can help you document your plan to create sexual behavior that will help you achieve sexual fulfillment and to avoid sexual behavior that hinders you in finding sexual fulfillment. Finally, the **Sexual Fulfillment Worksheet** can help provide positive and negative feedback regarding your effort.

In my experience as a marriage counselor I have found that when couples understand the five stages of the sexual experience and help each other achieve these stages when they make love, they usually find sexual fulfillment. This is because the process follows my Policy of Joint Agreement (*Never do anything without an enthusiastic agreement between you and your spouse*). It's very difficult, if not impossible, to share the stages of sexual experience during lovemaking unless both partners have learned to avoid gaining sexual pleasure at the other's expense. When it is *mutually* enjoyable, my Policy of Joint Agreement is being followed, and that's when couples find just about everything fulfilling, including sex.

Note: You may need multiple copies of these forms, so be sure to photocopy them rather than writing in the book.

Sexual Experience Inventory

The sexual experience divides into five stages: (1) willingness, (2) arousal, (3) plateau, (4) climax, and (5) recovery. The frst stage, willingness, gets the ball rolling. His willingness is usually motivated by testosterone-inspired sexual desire. But her willingness usually requires a combination of being emotionally connected to him and anticipating an enjoyable sexual experience with him. During arousal a man and woman begin to sense sexual feelings. His penis usually becomes erect, and her vagina usually begins to secrete fluid. If a man's penis and a woman's clitoris are stimulated properly, or if other sexually stimulating steps are taken, they pass into the plateau stage. In this stage sexual feelings are more intense and pleasurable. His penis becomes very hard and her vagina contracts, providing greater resistance and a heightened sexual sensation during intercourse. The climax, which usually lasts only a few seconds, is the peak of the sexual experience, with the most intense and pleasurable sensation. At this time the penis ejects semen in bursts (ejaculation), and the vagina alternately contracts and releases several times. Most women who wish to repeat a climax can continue experiencing them almost indefinitely, while most men cannot. The recovery stage follows, in which both partners feel peaceful and relaxed. The penis becomes soft, and the vagina, no longer secreting lubricating fluid, relaxes.

Please answer the following questions to provide information regarding your understanding of your sexual experience and your ability to create that experience. If your answers require more space, use and attach a separate sheet of paper.

Sexual Willingness

If you have experienced sexual willingness in the past, answer questions 1–4. If you have never experienced sexual willingness, skip to question 5.

1. How often do you experience sexual willingness?

    _____ times each day/week/month/year.
    (write number)   (circle one)

2. Describe the conditions that tend to create sexual willingness for you.

    _____

    _____

    _____

3. Are you more likely to experience sexual willingness when your spouse is with you or when he/she is not with you? Why?

    _____

    _____

4. If you have difficulty experiencing sexual willingness in the presence of your spouse, are you willing to create a plan with your spouse that may help you overcome that difficulty? When would you be willing to start planning?

_____

_____

5. If you have never experienced sexual willingness, are you willing to consult a qualified sex therapist to help you learn to create that experience? When would you be willing to begin?

_____

_____

Sexual Arousal

If you have experienced sexual arousal in the past, answer questions 1–4. If you have never experienced sexual arousal, skip to question 5.

1. How often do you experience sexual arousal?

_____ times each day/week/month/year.
   (write number)   (circle one)

2. Describe the conditions that tend to create sexual arousal for you.

_____

_____

_____

3. Are you more likely to experience sexual arousal when your spouse is with you or when he/she is not with you? Why?

_____

_____

4. If you have difficulty experiencing sexual arousal in the presence of your spouse, are you willing to create a plan with your spouse that may help you overcome that difficulty? When would you be willing to start planning?

_____

_____

5. If you have never experienced sexual arousal, are you willing to consult a qualified sex therapist to help you learn to create that experience? When would you be willing to begin?

_____

_____

Sexual Plateau

If you have experienced sexual plateau in the past, answer questions 1–4. If you have never experienced sexual plateau, skip to question 5.

1. How often do you experience sexual plateau?

_____ times each day/week/month/year.
(write number)   (circle one)

2. Describe the conditions that tend to create sexual plateau for you.

_____

_____

_____

3. Are you more likely to experience sexual plateau when your spouse is with you or when he/she is not with you? Why?

_____

_____

4. If you have difficulty experiencing sexual plateau in the presence of your spouse, are you willing to create a plan with your spouse that may help you overcome that difficulty? When would you be willing to start planning?

_____

_____

5. If you have never experienced sexual plateau, are you willing to consult a qualified sex therapist to help you learn to create that experience? When would you be willing to begin?

_____

_____

Sexual Climax

If you have experienced sexual climax in the past, answer questions 1–4. If you have never experienced sexual climax, skip to question 5.

1. How often do you experience sexual climax?

_____ times each day/week/month/year.
(write number)   (circle one)

2. Describe the conditions that tend to create sexual climax for you.

_____

_____

_____

3. Are you more likely to experience sexual climax when your spouse is with you or when he/she is not with you? Why?

_____

_____

4. If you have difficulty experiencing sexual climax in the presence of your spouse, are you willing to create a plan with your spouse that may help you overcome that difficulty? When would you be willing to start planning?

_____

_____

5. If you have never experienced sexual climax, are you willing to consult a qualified sex therapist to help you learn to create that experience? When would you be willing to begin?

_____

_____

Sexual Recovery

Unlike the other three stages of sexual experience, sexual recovery usually follows sexual climax naturally and effortlessly. But sometimes this experience is thwarted or incomplete. Answer the following questions to help understand your sexual recovery. If you have never experienced the other sexual stages, skip this section.

1. How often do you experience sexual recovery?

_____ times each day/week/month/year.
(write number)   (circle one)

2. Describe the conditions that tend to create sexual recovery for you.

_____

_____

_____

3. Are you more likely to experience sexual recovery when your spouse is with you or when he/she is not with you? Why?

_____

_____

4. If you have difficulty experiencing sexual recovery in the presence of your spouse, are you willing to create a plan with your spouse that may help you overcome that difficulty? When would you be willing to start planning?

_____

_____

5. Please add any information that may help in gaining an understanding of the stages of your sexual experiences.

_____

_____

_____

_____

_____

_____

Strategy to Discover the Five Stages
of Sexual Experience

∙ ∙

This form is designed to help you create a strategy to discover the five stages of sexual experience when you and your spouse make love. Complete each section to provide yourself with documentation of the process you used to select a strategy.

∙ ∙

1. After you complete the **Sexual Experience Inventory**, describe the stages of sexual experience that you have difficulty experiencing with your spouse.

   _____

   _____

   _____

   _____

2. Describe your plan to experience the sexual stages listed in question 1. Be certain that this plan is made with your spouse's enthusiastic support. Include a deadline to overcome your difficulty.

   _____

   _____

   _____

   _____

   _____

   _____

   _____

3. If your plan does not succeed within your designated time limit, will you agree to seek professional help to overcome this difficulty? How will you go about finding that help?

   _____

   _____

   _____

   _____

   _____

   _____

   _____

Sexual Experience Worksheet

· ·

This worksheet applies to the following stage of sexual experience: _____

_____

  Please list all instances of your effort to gain this stage of sexual experience. Indicate whether or not the stage was achieved and whether or not conditions that help you create this experience were met.

· ·

	Day	Date	Time	Circumstances
1.	_____	_____	_____	_____
2.	_____	_____	_____	_____
3.	_____	_____	_____	_____
4.	_____	_____	_____	_____
5.	_____	_____	_____	_____
6.	_____	_____	_____	_____
7.	_____	_____	_____	_____
8.	_____	_____	_____	_____

Sexual Fulfillment Inventory

*This form should be used only when you have learned to share the five stages
of sexual experience but still find yourself sexually unfulfilled.*

Under the heading Sexual Habits to Create, please name and describe the types of sexual behavior that you would like from your spouse. For example, if you would like your spouse to have sexual intercourse with you more often, you should simply indicate how often and under which circumstances you would enjoy sexual intercourse.

If your spouse engages in sexual behavior that you find annoying or inappropriate for your needs, name and describe that behavior under the heading Sexual Habits to Avoid. You may find that it isn't the behavior itself that you consider inappropriate, but rather the time and place that bother you. If that's the case, explain that clearly in your description and include the appropriate circumstances under Sexual Habits to Create. If you need more space for your descriptions or would like to list more habits than the form allows, use another sheet of paper and attach it to this form.

You and your spouse should complete separate **Sexual Fulfillment Inventories**. After reviewing each other's tastes in sex, try to develop sexual habits that you both want to create, and try to avoid habits that either of you finds annoying.

Sexual Habits to Create

1. _____

   _____

   _____

2. _____

   _____

   _____

3. _____

   _____

   _____

4. _____

   _____

   _____

5. _____
_____
_____

6. _____
_____
_____

Sexual Habits to Avoid

1. _____
_____
_____

2. _____
_____
_____

3. _____
_____
_____

4. _____
_____
_____

5. _____
_____
_____

6. _____
_____
_____

Strategy to Meet the Need of Sexual Fulfillment

This form is designed to help you create a strategy to meet your spouse's need for sexual fulfillment. It is to be used only when you and your spouse have learned to share the five stages of the sexual experience when you make love but your spouse is still sexually unfulfilled. Complete each section to provide yourself with documentation of the process you used to select a strategy.

1. Referring to your spouse's completed **Sexual Fulfillment Inventory**, describe sexual behavior that your spouse would like you to learn.

_____
_____
_____
_____
_____
_____

2. Describe your plan to learn the sexual behavior listed in question 1. Be certain that this plan is made with the enthusiastic agreement of both you and your spouse. Include a deadline to learn this sexual behavior.

_____
_____
_____
_____
_____
_____

3. If your plan does not succeed within your designated time limit, will you agree to seek professional help to learn this sexual behavior? How will you go about finding that help?

_____
_____
_____
_____
_____
_____

4. Describe the sexual behavior that your spouse would like you to avoid.

_____

_____

_____

_____

_____

_____

5. Describe your plan to avoid sexual behavior listed in question 4. Be certain that this plan is made with the enthusiastic agreement of both you and your spouse. Include a deadline to avoid this behavior.

_____

_____

_____

_____

_____

_____

6. If your plan to avoid unwanted sexual behavior does not succeed within your designated time limit, will you agree to seek professional help to avoid this behavior? How will you go about finding that help?

_____

_____

_____

_____

_____

Sexual Fulfillment Worksheet

• •

Please list all instances of your spouse's sexual behavior and your emotional reaction. If you find your spouse emotionally upset with your honest reactions, or if you are reluctant to provide honest reactions, seek professional supervision.

• •

	Day	Date	Time	Type of Sexual Behavior and Your Reaction
1.	_____	_____	_____	_____
2.	_____	_____	_____	_____
3.	_____	_____	_____	_____
4.	_____	_____	_____	_____
5.	_____	_____	_____	_____
6.	_____	_____	_____	_____
7.	_____	_____	_____	_____
8.	_____	_____	_____	_____

Learning to Meet the Need of Conversation

Conversation is the way we communicate with each other to solve many of our problems. For many people, especially women, conversation also meets an emotional need. These people will create a subject to talk about just for the sake of talking. It's the conversation itself that meets their need and makes them feel good.

People who don't experience a need for conversation often press those that do for a "reason" for the conversation. "Why did you call?" "Have we exhausted that subject yet?" "Where is this conversation headed?"

They don't realize that their partners in conversation enjoy it for the sake of the conversation. When that's the case, conversation can deposit mountains of love units when it's done correctly.

In chapter 5 of *His Needs, Her Needs*, I encourage couples to become skilled in depositing love units when they talk to each other. "Friends" of good conversation deposit love units, but "enemies" withdraw them. The friends of good conversation are (1) developing interest in each other's favorite topics, (2) giving each other equal time to talk, (3) using conversation to inform, investigate, and understand each other, and (4) giving undivided attention. The enemies of good conversation are (1) trying to get one's way at the other's expense, (2) using conversation to punish each other, (3) trying to force agreement with one's way of thinking, and (4) dwelling on mistakes of the past or present.

If you or your spouse has identified conversation as an important emotional need, you should not only set aside time specifically for conversation, but you should also be certain that your conversation is mutually enjoyable.

I've designed the **Friends and Enemies of Good Conversation Inventory** to help you determine which habits you should create and which ones you should avoid in your conversation. Remember, the friends make you feel good about the conversation, and the enemies make you feel bad. You can add to my list of friends and enemies of good conversation as you identify them in the way you and your spouse feel when you talk to each other.

After the inventory is completed, the **Strategy to Meet the Need of Conversation** can be helpful in documenting your plan to create friends and avoid enemies of good conversation.

I recommend that your plan include "practice conversations," times set aside to practice conversational skills. As you talk to each other, each of you should use the **Friends and Enemies of Good Conversation Worksheet** to list instances of the friends and enemies. After the conversation, compare worksheets. Don't challenge each other's judgments, but rather accept the evaluation of your spouse and renew your commitment to create the friends and eliminate the enemies in your next conversation.

You may also use the worksheet after a normal conversation when your spouse has made an effort to use a friend, or made the mistake of using an enemy, of good conversation. If you find yourselves arguing about each other's interpretations of the friends and enemies, remember that friends always make your spouse feel good and enemies make your spouse feel bad. Your spouse knows if you are using friends or enemies because your spouse feels the effect of your conversation. He/she is the only one who can make the judgment.

Conversation is about the only way couples can solve marital problems. So when they let enemies raise their ugly heads, problems remain unsolved, and love units are lost in the trying. Remember, you'll get nowhere unless you can discuss problems in a pleasant and encouraging way. Using conversation to vent your frustration may help you feel better momentarily, but it will make your problem more difficult to solve in the long run. When the process of problem-solving enlists the friends of good conversation, solutions abound and romantic love remains secure.

Note: You may need multiple copies of these forms, so be sure to photocopy them rather than writing in the book.

Friends and Enemies of
Good Conversation Inventory

The conversations you have with your spouse can be either enjoyable or unpleasant. You will tend to have a pleasant conversation when your spouse (1) develops an interest in your favorite topics of conversation, (2) balances the conversation, (3) uses the conversation to inform, investigate, and understand you, or (4) gives you undivided attention when he/she talks to you. These are some of the friends of good conversation.

You will tend to have an unpleasant conversation when your spouse (1) tries to get his or her way at your expense, (2) uses conversation to punish you, (3) tries to force his or her way of thinking on you, or (4) dwells on your mistakes of the past or present. These are some of the enemies of good conversation.

Under the heading Friends of Good Conversation to Create, please name and describe new conversational habits that you would like your spouse to develop. For example, you could simply list one or more of the friends of good conversation mentioned above, or you could add others that would improve conversation for you. You could even indicate that more time for conversation is needed.

If your spouse engages in conversational habits that you find annoying or inappropriate for your needs, name and describe that behavior under the heading Enemies of Good Conversation to Avoid. You may find that it isn't the behavior itself that you consider inappropriate, but rather the time and place that bother you. If that's the case, explain that clearly in your description and include the appropriate circumstances under Friends of Good Conversation to Create. If you need more space for your descriptions or would like to list more friends and enemies than the form allows, use another sheet of paper and attach it to this form.

Since conversation is interactive (one of you can't engage in meaningful conversation without the other participating), you and your spouse should complete separate **Friends and Enemies of Good Conversation Inventories**. After reviewing each other's tastes in conversation, try to develop habits of conversation that you both want to create, and try to avoid habits that either of you finds annoying.

Friends of Good Conversation to Create

1. _____
   _____
   _____

2. _____
   _____
   _____

3. _____

_____

_____

4. _____

_____

_____

5. _____

_____

_____

Enemies of Good Conversation to Avoid

1. _____

_____

_____

2. _____

_____

_____

3. _____

_____

_____

4. _____

_____

_____

5. _____

_____

_____

Strategy to Meet the Need of Conversation

This form is designed to help you create a strategy to meet your spouse's need for conversation. Complete each section to provide yourself with documentation of the process you used to select a strategy.

1. Referring to your spouse's completed **Friends and Enemies of Good Conversation Inventory**, describe conversational behavior that your spouse would like you to learn.

   _____

   _____

   _____

   _____

   _____

   _____

2. Describe your plan to learn the conversational behavior listed in question 1. Be certain that this plan is made with the enthusiastic agreement of both you and your spouse. Include a deadline to learn this conversational behavior.

   _____

   _____

   _____

   _____

   _____

   _____

3. If your plan does not succeed within your designated time limit, will you agree to seek professional help to learn appropriate conversational behavior? How will you go about finding that help?

   _____

   _____

   _____

   _____

   _____

   _____

4. Describe the conversational behavior that your spouse would like you to avoid.

_____

_____

_____

_____

_____

_____

5. Describe your plan to avoid the conversational behavior listed in question 4. Be certain that this plan is made with the enthusiastic agreement of both you and your spouse. Include a deadline to avoid this behavior.

_____

_____

_____

_____

_____

_____

6. If your plan to avoid unwanted conversational behavior does not succeed within your designated time limit, will you agree to seek professional help to avoid this behavior? How will you go about finding that help?

_____

_____

_____

_____

_____

_____

Friends and Enemies
of Good Conversation Worksheet

Each time you and your spouse have a conversation that is over one minute in length, take a moment to evaluate its quality. As a reminder:

The friends of good conversation: (1) developing an interest in each other's favorite topics of conversation, (2) balancing the conversation, (3) using the conversation to inform, investigate, and understand each other, and (4) giving each other undivided attention. Add to this list any other conversational habits that you want your spouse to develop:

The enemies of good conversation: (1) trying to get one's way at the other's expense, (2) using conversation to punish, (3) trying to force agreement with one's way of thinking, and (4) dwelling on mistakes of the past or present. Add to this list any other conversational habits that you want your spouse to avoid:

Please list the instances of friends and enemies of good conversation that were made *by your spouse* during the conversation. Your spouse is to complete a similar worksheet for his/her evaluation of your conversation. After the conversation, exchange worksheets and acknowledge each other's evaluations. *Do not try to defend yourself if you do not agree with your spouse's evaluation.* Accept it, and express willingness to improve the conversation at the next opportunity.

Day	Date	Time	Friend and/or Enemy of Good Conversation
1. _____	_____	_____	_____
			_____
			_____
			_____
2. _____	_____	_____	_____
			_____
			_____
			_____
3. _____	_____	_____	_____
			_____
			_____
			_____

	Day	Date	Time	Friend and/or Enemy of Good Conversation
4.	_____	_____	_____	_____
				_____
				_____
				_____
5.	_____	_____	_____	_____
				_____
				_____
				_____
6.	_____	_____	_____	_____
				_____
				_____
				_____
7.	_____	_____	_____	_____
				_____
				_____
				_____
8.	_____	_____	_____	_____
				_____
				_____
				_____
9.	_____	_____	_____	_____
				_____
				_____
				_____
10.	_____	_____	_____	_____
				_____
				_____
				_____
11.	_____	_____	_____	_____
				_____
				_____
				_____
				_____

Learning to Meet the Need
of Recreational Companionship

It's all too obvious that when you spend recreational time together, you have a great opportunity to deposit love units in each other's Love Banks. It simply makes good sense for couples to take every opportunity to share recreational experiences because it's such an easy way to sustain romantic love.

For some, especially men, recreation is not only an enjoyable diversion, but it also meets an important emotional need. It's something that often "keeps them going." For these people, recreational companionship is particularly satisfying. Those that share their favorite recreational activities with them build massive Love Bank accounts, particularly if they're of the opposite sex.

One of my objectives in writing chapter 6 of *His Needs, Her Needs* was to encourage couples to spend most, if not all, of their recreational time together. It's one of the most efficient and effective ways to build romantic love. If your spouse listed recreational companionship as one of his/her top five emotional needs, then you have even greater reason to follow my advice.

Most couples share favorite recreational activities during courtship. It's an important reason that they fall in love. But after marriage a host of circumstances prevents these activities from being shared, and before long they find it easier to engage in recreational activities independently. Because their wives don't join them anyway, the men pick activities that don't take their wives' feelings into account. The women, meanwhile, seek out their favorite activities, which may be totally unpleasant to their husbands. Eventually, such couples realize that they've "drifted apart" and wonder why. They simply failed to consider each other in selecting recreational activities. That failure almost always will lead to incompatibility.

How do you get back on track after you find yourselves in this mess? If you do not enjoy your spouse's favorite activity, love units are withdrawn from *your* Love Bank whenever you try to join him/her. As your spouse gains love for you, you lose love for your spouse. Since I make it clear that you should not engage in any activity that makes either of you feel bad (Policy of Joint Agreement), I suggest that you abandon incompatible activities and search for recreational activities that you both enjoy. Then both of you can deposit love units.

The **Recreational Enjoyment Inventory** is designed to help you discover these mutually enjoyable activities. One hundred twenty-two activities are listed, with space to add other favorites. You and your spouse are to rate all the activities for enjoyment. Only those activities with high ratings by both of you are to be selected for joint participation. Recreational activities that cannot be enjoyed together are to be discontinued.

While the strategy for achieving recreational companionship should be fairly easy to implement, I have included the **Strategy to Meet the Need of Recreational Companionship** form so that you can document your plan. Try to spend almost all of your recreational time together. The myth that men and women simply cannot ever enjoy the same activities is rubbish. If you have a willingness to try something new, and give yourselves a chance to learn necessary skills and develop understanding, you'll prove to yourselves that you have a lot more in common than you think.

As you try different activities, the **Recreational Companionship Worksheet** will be helpful in documenting progress toward achieving compatibility. Some activities will click as soon as you try them, while others may take a while to discover whether or not you'll be able to make a good adjustment. In the end, abandon those activities that one of you does not enjoy.

Why engage in recreational activities that cannot be shared and enjoyed by your spouse? Out of the thousands of activities that you can enjoy, why pick the few that your spouse can't enjoy? Why not find those you can share? The pleasure you may receive from your independent activities is at the expense of your romantic love. Don't do it. It's not worth the price.

Note: You may need multiple copies of these forms, so be sure to photocopy them rather than writing in the book.

Recreational Enjoyment Inventory

Please indicate how much you enjoy, or think you might enjoy, each recreational activity listed below. In the space provided by each activity, under the appropriate column (husband's or wife's), circle one of the following numbers to reflect your feelings: 3 = very enjoyable; 2 = enjoyable; 1 = somewhat enjoyable; 0 = no feelings one way or the other; -1 = somewhat unpleasant; -2 = unpleasant; -3 = very unpleasant. Add to the list, in the spaces provided, activities that you would enjoy that are not listed. In the third column, add the ratings of both you and your spouse *only if both ratings are positive*. The activities with the highest sum are those that you should select when planning recreational time together.

Activity	Husband's Rating	Wife's Rating	Total Rating
Acting	-3 -2 -1 0 1 2 3	-3 -2 -1 0 1 2 3	_____
Aerobic exercise	-3 -2 -1 0 1 2 3	-3 -2 -1 0 1 2 3	_____
Amusement parks	-3 -2 -1 0 1 2 3	-3 -2 -1 0 1 2 3	_____
Antique collecting	-3 -2 -1 0 1 2 3	-3 -2 -1 0 1 2 3	_____
Archery	-3 -2 -1 0 1 2 3	-3 -2 -1 0 1 2 3	_____
Astronomy	-3 -2 -1 0 1 2 3	-3 -2 -1 0 1 2 3	_____
Auto customizing	-3 -2 -1 0 1 2 3	-3 -2 -1 0 1 2 3	_____
Auto racing (watching)	-3 -2 -1 0 1 2 3	-3 -2 -1 0 1 2 3	_____
Badminton	-3 -2 -1 0 1 2 3	-3 -2 -1 0 1 2 3	_____
Baseball (watching)	-3 -2 -1 0 1 2 3	-3 -2 -1 0 1 2 3	_____
Baseball (playing)	-3 -2 -1 0 1 2 3	-3 -2 -1 0 1 2 3	_____
Basketball (watching)	-3 -2 -1 0 1 2 3	-3 -2 -1 0 1 2 3	_____
Basketball (playing)	-3 -2 -1 0 1 2 3	-3 -2 -1 0 1 2 3	_____
Bible study	-3 -2 -1 0 1 2 3	-3 -2 -1 0 1 2 3	_____
Bicycling	-3 -2 -1 0 1 2 3	-3 -2 -1 0 1 2 3	_____
Boating	-3 -2 -1 0 1 2 3	-3 -2 -1 0 1 2 3	_____
Bodybuilding	-3 -2 -1 0 1 2 3	-3 -2 -1 0 1 2 3	_____
Bowling	-3 -2 -1 0 1 2 3	-3 -2 -1 0 1 2 3	_____
Boxing (watching)	-3 -2 -1 0 1 2 3	-3 -2 -1 0 1 2 3	_____
Bridge	-3 -2 -1 0 1 2 3	-3 -2 -1 0 1 2 3	_____
Camping	-3 -2 -1 0 1 2 3	-3 -2 -1 0 1 2 3	_____
Canasta	-3 -2 -1 0 1 2 3	-3 -2 -1 0 1 2 3	_____
Canoeing	-3 -2 -1 0 1 2 3	-3 -2 -1 0 1 2 3	_____
Checkers	-3 -2 -1 0 1 2 3	-3 -2 -1 0 1 2 3	_____
Chess	-3 -2 -1 0 1 2 3	-3 -2 -1 0 1 2 3	_____
Church services	-3 -2 -1 0 1 2 3	-3 -2 -1 0 1 2 3	_____
Coin collecting	-3 -2 -1 0 1 2 3	-3 -2 -1 0 1 2 3	_____

Activity	Husband's Rating	Wife's Rating	Total Rating
Computer programming	–3 –2 –1 0 1 2 3	–3 –2 –1 0 1 2 3	_____
Computer games	–3 –2 –1 0 1 2 3	–3 –2 –1 0 1 2 3	_____
Computer _____	–3 –2 –1 0 1 2 3	–3 –2 –1 0 1 2 3	_____
Concerts (rock music)	–3 –2 –1 0 1 2 3	–3 –2 –1 0 1 2 3	_____
Concerts (classical music)	–3 –2 –1 0 1 2 3	–3 –2 –1 0 1 2 3	_____
Concerts (country music)	–3 –2 –1 0 1 2 3	–3 –2 –1 0 1 2 3	_____
Cribbage	–3 –2 –1 0 1 2 3	–3 –2 –1 0 1 2 3	_____
Croquet	–3 –2 –1 0 1 2 3	–3 –2 –1 0 1 2 3	_____
Dancing (ballroom)	–3 –2 –1 0 1 2 3	–3 –2 –1 0 1 2 3	_____
Dancing (square)	–3 –2 –1 0 1 2 3	–3 –2 –1 0 1 2 3	_____
Dancing (rock)	–3 –2 –1 0 1 2 3	–3 –2 –1 0 1 2 3	_____
Dancing (_____)	–3 –2 –1 0 1 2 3	–3 –2 –1 0 1 2 3	_____
Dining out	–3 –2 –1 0 1 2 3	–3 –2 –1 0 1 2 3	_____
Fishing	–3 –2 –1 0 1 2 3	–3 –2 –1 0 1 2 3	_____
Flying (as pilot)	–3 –2 –1 0 1 2 3	–3 –2 –1 0 1 2 3	_____
Flying (as passenger)	–3 –2 –1 0 1 2 3	–3 –2 –1 0 1 2 3	_____
Football (watching)	–3 –2 –1 0 1 2 3	–3 –2 –1 0 1 2 3	_____
Football (playing)	–3 –2 –1 0 1 2 3	–3 –2 –1 0 1 2 3	_____
Gardening	–3 –2 –1 0 1 2 3	–3 –2 –1 0 1 2 3	_____
Genealogical research	–3 –2 –1 0 1 2 3	–3 –2 –1 0 1 2 3	_____
Golf	–3 –2 –1 0 1 2 3	–3 –2 –1 0 1 2 3	_____
Ham radio	–3 –2 –1 0 1 2 3	–3 –2 –1 0 1 2 3	_____
Handball	–3 –2 –1 0 1 2 3	–3 –2 –1 0 1 2 3	_____
Hiking	–3 –2 –1 0 1 2 3	–3 –2 –1 0 1 2 3	_____
Hockey (watching)	–3 –2 –1 0 1 2 3	–3 –2 –1 0 1 2 3	_____
Hockey (playing)	–3 –2 –1 0 1 2 3	–3 –2 –1 0 1 2 3	_____
Horseback riding	–3 –2 –1 0 1 2 3	–3 –2 –1 0 1 2 3	_____
Horse shows (watching)	–3 –2 –1 0 1 2 3	–3 –2 –1 0 1 2 3	_____
Horse racing	–3 –2 –1 0 1 2 3	–3 –2 –1 0 1 2 3	_____
Horseshoe pitching	–3 –2 –1 0 1 2 3	–3 –2 –1 0 1 2 3	_____
Hot air ballooning	–3 –2 –1 0 1 2 3	–3 –2 –1 0 1 2 3	_____
Hunting	–3 –2 –1 0 1 2 3	–3 –2 –1 0 1 2 3	_____
Ice fishing	–3 –2 –1 0 1 2 3	–3 –2 –1 0 1 2 3	_____
Ice skating	–3 –2 –1 0 1 2 3	–3 –2 –1 0 1 2 3	_____
Jogging	–3 –2 –1 0 1 2 3	–3 –2 –1 0 1 2 3	_____
Judo	–3 –2 –1 0 1 2 3	–3 –2 –1 0 1 2 3	_____
Karate	–3 –2 –1 0 1 2 3	–3 –2 –1 0 1 2 3	_____
Knitting	–3 –2 –1 0 1 2 3	–3 –2 –1 0 1 2 3	_____

Activity	Husband's Rating	Wife's Rating	Total Rating
Metalwork	−3 −2 −1 0 1 2 3	−3 −2 −1 0 1 2 3	_____
Model building	−3 −2 −1 0 1 2 3	−3 −2 −1 0 1 2 3	_____
Monopoly	−3 −2 −1 0 1 2 3	−3 −2 −1 0 1 2 3	_____
Mountain climbing	−3 −2 −1 0 1 2 3	−3 −2 −1 0 1 2 3	_____
Movies	−3 −2 −1 0 1 2 3	−3 −2 −1 0 1 2 3	_____
Museums	−3 −2 −1 0 1 2 3	−3 −2 −1 0 1 2 3	_____
Opera	−3 −2 −1 0 1 2 3	−3 −2 −1 0 1 2 3	_____
Painting	−3 −2 −1 0 1 2 3	−3 −2 −1 0 1 2 3	_____
Photography	−3 −2 −1 0 1 2 3	−3 −2 −1 0 1 2 3	_____
Pinochle	−3 −2 −1 0 1 2 3	−3 −2 −1 0 1 2 3	_____
Plays	−3 −2 −1 0 1 2 3	−3 −2 −1 0 1 2 3	_____
Poetry (writing)	−3 −2 −1 0 1 2 3	−3 −2 −1 0 1 2 3	_____
Polo (watching)	−3 −2 −1 0 1 2 3	−3 −2 −1 0 1 2 3	_____
Pool (or billiards)	−3 −2 −1 0 1 2 3	−3 −2 −1 0 1 2 3	_____
Quilting	−3 −2 −1 0 1 2 3	−3 −2 −1 0 1 2 3	_____
Racquetball	−3 −2 −1 0 1 2 3	−3 −2 −1 0 1 2 3	_____
Remodeling (home)	−3 −2 −1 0 1 2 3	−3 −2 −1 0 1 2 3	_____
Rock collecting	−3 −2 −1 0 1 2 3	−3 −2 −1 0 1 2 3	_____
Roller-skating	−3 −2 −1 0 1 2 3	−3 −2 −1 0 1 2 3	_____
Rowing	−3 −2 −1 0 1 2 3	−3 −2 −1 0 1 2 3	_____
Rummy	−3 −2 −1 0 1 2 3	−3 −2 −1 0 1 2 3	_____
Sailing	−3 −2 −1 0 1 2 3	−3 −2 −1 0 1 2 3	_____
Sculpting	−3 −2 −1 0 1 2 3	−3 −2 −1 0 1 2 3	_____
Shooting (skeet, trap)	−3 −2 −1 0 1 2 3	−3 −2 −1 0 1 2 3	_____
Shooting (pistol)	−3 −2 −1 0 1 2 3	−3 −2 −1 0 1 2 3	_____
Shopping (clothes)	−3 −2 −1 0 1 2 3	−3 −2 −1 0 1 2 3	_____
Shopping (groceries)	−3 −2 −1 0 1 2 3	−3 −2 −1 0 1 2 3	_____
Shopping (vehicles)	−3 −2 −1 0 1 2 3	−3 −2 −1 0 1 2 3	_____
Shopping (_____)	−3 −2 −1 0 1 2 3	−3 −2 −1 0 1 2 3	_____
Shuffleboard	−3 −2 −1 0 1 2 3	−3 −2 −1 0 1 2 3	_____
Sightseeing	−3 −2 −1 0 1 2 3	−3 −2 −1 0 1 2 3	_____
Singing	−3 −2 −1 0 1 2 3	−3 −2 −1 0 1 2 3	_____
Skiing (water)	−3 −2 −1 0 1 2 3	−3 −2 −1 0 1 2 3	_____
Skiing (downhill)	−3 −2 −1 0 1 2 3	−3 −2 −1 0 1 2 3	_____
Skiing (cross-country)	−3 −2 −1 0 1 2 3	−3 −2 −1 0 1 2 3	_____
Skin diving (snorkeling)	−3 −2 −1 0 1 2 3	−3 −2 −1 0 1 2 3	_____
Skydiving	−3 −2 −1 0 1 2 3	−3 −2 −1 0 1 2 3	_____
Snowmobiling	−3 −2 −1 0 1 2 3	−3 −2 −1 0 1 2 3	_____

Activity	Husband's Rating	Wife's Rating	Total Rating
Softball (watching)	–3 –2 –1 0 1 2 3	–3 –2 –1 0 1 2 3	_____
Softball (playing)	–3 –2 –1 0 1 2 3	–3 –2 –1 0 1 2 3	_____
Spearfishing	–3 –2 –1 0 1 2 3	–3 –2 –1 0 1 2 3	_____
Stamp collecting	–3 –2 –1 0 1 2 3	–3 –2 –1 0 1 2 3	_____
Surfing	–3 –2 –1 0 1 2 3	–3 –2 –1 0 1 2 3	_____
Swimming	–3 –2 –1 0 1 2 3	–3 –2 –1 0 1 2 3	_____
Table tennis	–3 –2 –1 0 1 2 3	–3 –2 –1 0 1 2 3	_____
Taxidermy	–3 –2 –1 0 1 2 3	–3 –2 –1 0 1 2 3	_____
Television	–3 –2 –1 0 1 2 3	–3 –2 –1 0 1 2 3	_____
Tennis	–3 –2 –1 0 1 2 3	–3 –2 –1 0 1 2 3	_____
Tobogganing	–3 –2 –1 0 1 2 3	–3 –2 –1 0 1 2 3	_____
Video games	–3 –2 –1 0 1 2 3	–3 –2 –1 0 1 2 3	_____
Video production	–3 –2 –1 0 1 2 3	–3 –2 –1 0 1 2 3	_____
Video movies (watching)	–3 –2 –1 0 1 2 3	–3 –2 –1 0 1 2 3	
Volleyball	–3 –2 –1 0 1 2 3	–3 –2 –1 0 1 2 3	_____
Weaving	–3 –2 –1 0 1 2 3	–3 –2 –1 0 1 2 3	_____
Woodworking	–3 –2 –1 0 1 2 3	–3 –2 –1 0 1 2 3	_____
Wrestling (watching)	–3 –2 –1 0 1 2 3	–3 –2 –1 0 1 2 3	_____
Yachting	–3 –2 –1 0 1 2 3	–3 –2 –1 0 1 2 3	_____
_____	–3 –2 –1 0 1 2 3	–3 –2 –1 0 1 2 3	_____
_____	–3 –2 –1 0 1 2 3	–3 –2 –1 0 1 2 3	_____
_____	–3 –2 –1 0 1 2 3	–3 –2 –1 0 1 2 3	_____
_____	–3 –2 –1 0 1 2 3	–3 –2 –1 0 1 2 3	_____
_____	–3 –2 –1 0 1 2 3	–3 –2 –1 0 1 2 3	_____
_____	–3 –2 –1 0 1 2 3	–3 –2 –1 0 1 2 3	_____
_____	–3 –2 –1 0 1 2 3	–3 –2 –1 0 1 2 3	_____
_____	–3 –2 –1 0 1 2 3	–3 –2 –1 0 1 2 3	_____
_____	–3 –2 –1 0 1 2 3	–3 –2 –1 0 1 2 3	_____
_____	–3 –2 –1 0 1 2 3	–3 –2 –1 0 1 2 3	_____
_____	–3 –2 –1 0 1 2 3	–3 –2 –1 0 1 2 3	_____
_____	–3 –2 –1 0 1 2 3	–3 –2 –1 0 1 2 3	_____
_____	–3 –2 –1 0 1 2 3	–3 –2 –1 0 1 2 3	_____
_____	–3 –2 –1 0 1 2 3	–3 –2 –1 0 1 2 3	_____
_____	–3 –2 –1 0 1 2 3	–3 –2 –1 0 1 2 3	_____
_____	–3 –2 –1 0 1 2 3	–3 –2 –1 0 1 2 3	_____

Strategy to Meet the Need
of Recreational Companionship

This form is designed to help you create a strategy to meet your spouse's need for recreational companionship. Complete each section to provide yourself with documentation of the process you used to select a strategy.

1. After you complete the **Recreational Enjoyment Inventory**, list the recreational activities that both you and your spouse enjoy.

   _____

   _____

   _____

   _____

   _____

   _____

2. Describe your plan to engage in these recreational activities together. Be certain that this plan is made with the enthusiastic support of both you and your spouse. Include a deadline to be spending your recreational time together.

   _____

   _____

   _____

   _____

   _____

   _____

3. If your plan does not succeed within your designated time limit, will you agree to seek professional help to spend recreational time with your spouse? How will you go about finding that help?

   _____

   _____

   _____

   _____

   _____

   _____

Recreational Companionship Worksheet

Please list all recreational activities shared by you and your spouse, and describe your emotional reaction to the time you spent together. If you enjoyed the time together, explain what made it enjoyable. If you disliked the time together, explain what made it unpleasant. Try to avoid unpleasant aspects of your time together when you next engage in that activity. If you find your spouse emotionally upset with your honest reactions, or if you are reluctant to provide honest reactions, seek professional supervision.

	Day	Date	Time	Recreational Activity and Your Reaction
1.	_____	_____	_____	_____
				_____
				_____
2.	_____	_____	_____	_____
				_____
				_____
3.	_____	_____	_____	_____
				_____
				_____
4.	_____	_____	_____	_____
				_____
				_____
5.	_____	_____	_____	_____
				_____
				_____
6.	_____	_____	_____	_____
				_____
				_____
7.	_____	_____	_____	_____
				_____
				_____
8.	_____	_____	_____	_____
				_____
				_____
				_____

Learning to Meet the Need of Honesty and Openness

Honesty and openness in marriage have many practical advantages over dishonesty. If your spouse doesn't have the facts, how can you hope to solve problems together? When you give your spouse false information or no information about yourself, he/she is bound to make serious mistakes trying to make adjustments to accommodate you. Your dishonesty makes your own marital fulfillment much more difficult to achieve.

None of us wants to be lied to, but for some, especially women, honesty and openness is an emotional need. When this need is met, romantic love is much easier to sustain. But when it's unmet, it's a Love Buster and it destroys romantic love.

Honesty and openness as an emotional need are discussed in chapter 7 of *His Needs, Her Needs*, and dishonesty as a destructive habit is treated in chapter 6 of *Love Busters*. The procedure I follow to overcome the Love Buster dishonesty is the same as the one I follow to meet the emotional need for honesty. So I refer you to the forms used to overcome the Love Buster dishonesty, found in step three of this workbook. When dishonesty is overcome, honesty and openness result.

If you've already overcome all the Love Busters, including dishonesty, you will also be meeting your spouse's need for honesty and openness.

Learning to Meet the Need of Physical Attractiveness

When we were first married, most of us found our spouses physically attractive. In fact, most of our spouses *wanted* us to find them physically attractive. And we wanted our spouses to find us physically attractive. Prior to marriage most of us went to some trouble to develop and maintain attractive bodies. We exercised, watched our diet, selected our clothes carefully, and tried to be hygienically "nice to be near." If we failed to be attractive, we risked losing those we were crazy about.

But after marriage we have them hooked! We want them to love us for who we are rather than for what we look like, and for many, physical appearance takes a horrible turn. That's okay if physical appearance isn't one of our spouses' most important emotional needs, but if it's one of the top five, we're in deep trouble.

I discuss the need for physical attractiveness in chapter 8 of *His Needs, Her Needs*. It's a touchy subject, since, as I've mentioned, most of us come to *expect* our spouses to find us attractive. When we discover that they don't consider us as attractive as we once were, some of us are deeply offended. That's what makes it so difficult to communicate failure to meet this emotional need. If we are so offended by the revelation, our spouses might prefer to let this need go unmet rather than face the fact that the problem exists.

If your spouse has identified physical attractiveness as an unmet need, you have already passed that difficult hurdle of honesty, and you're in a great position to solve the problem. First, you need to know what changes in your physical appearance your spouse needs the most. The **Physical Appearance Inventory** helps provide that information.

Once you know which characteristics need changing, the **Strategy to Meet the Need of Physical Attractiveness** form can help you document your plan. One of these forms should be completed for each characteristic listed in the **Physical Appearance Inventory**. Some changes will be almost effortless, while others will require great discipline and commitment. Professional help may be required with a problem such as weight loss. If you need help, be certain that the professional you choose has an outstanding record of success. Beware of those who want to help but don't know how. Be particularly careful to avoid those who want you and your spouse to learn to accept your present state!

It's been my experience that the natural changes that occur in aging do not reduce attractiveness for most partners of the same age. The problem is usually in personal care and taste differences between partners. An effort to cater to the tastes of your spouse and be as attractive as possible usually does the trick.

Note: You may need multiple copies of these forms, so be sure to photocopy them rather than writing in the book.

Physical Appearance Inventory

Under the heading Characteristics of Attractiveness to Create, please name and describe the changes in physical appearance that you would like from your spouse. Include consideration of weight, physical fitness, clothing, hairstyle, physical hygiene (cleanliness), facial makeup (for women), and well-groomed eyebrows, mustache, and beard (for men). Add any other categories that you think would affect your spouse's attraction to you. Be as specific as you can in describing changes in physical appearance. If you need more space for your answers, use and attach a separate sheet of paper.

Characteristics of Attractiveness to Create

1. _____
   _____
   _____

2. _____
   _____
   _____

3. _____
   _____
   _____

4. _____
   _____
   _____

5. _____
   _____
   _____

6. _____
   _____
   _____

Strategy to Meet the Need
of Physical Attractiveness

. . . .

This form is designed to help you create a strategy to improve the following characteristic of physical attractiveness: _____

Complete each section of the worksheet to provide yourself with documentation of the process you used to select a strategy.

. . . .

1. Describe the physical characteristic that your spouse would like you to improve.

   _____
   _____
   _____
   _____

2. Describe your plan to improve the physical characteristic. Be certain that this plan is made with the enthusiastic agreement of both you and your spouse. Include a deadline to make this change.

   _____
   _____
   _____
   _____
   _____
   _____
   _____
   _____

3. If your plan does not succeed within your designated time limit, will you agree to seek professional help to improve this characteristic? How will you go about finding that help?

   _____
   _____
   _____
   _____
   _____
   _____

Learning to Meet the Need of Financial Support

The need for financial support, discussed in chapter 9 of *His Needs, Her Needs*, is usually selected by women as one of their five most important emotional needs. Men rarely indicate any need at all for financial support, although we may see this change in the future. But at present, this sex difference becomes obvious when you ask people, "Would you marry someone who would expect to be supported financially, who preferred doing something that didn't earn an income, such as raising his or her own children, or volunteering his or her services?" Today, most men would say "yes" and most women would say "no."

If a woman has a need for financial support, it makes sense that she'd object to supporting a man. How could her need be met if he expected her to support him? I've found that even among women who don't claim to have a need for financial support, the idea of supporting a man is often repulsive. These women expect men at least to divide living expenses with them. They usually feel "used" when they find themselves supporting men who have no desire to earn a living. From my perspective, this unwillingness to support men financially reflects a deep and pervasive emotional need for financial support. As women become more financially self-sufficient in our society, I don't expect their attitudes to change much regarding their financial support of unemployed men. We'll see if my hunch holds up.

Most men encourage their wives to find careers for their own personal fulfillment. If their wives choose not to earn a living and volunteer their skills, most men can live with that, but a man's failure to develop an income-producing career can lead to a marital disaster.

There are exceptions. If neither spouse has a need for financial support, neither objects to supporting the other. In these marriages, they either share living expenses from their individual incomes, or one works for an income for a while, and then the other works for a while. They usually don't "count" to see who's paying the most.

I've also witnessed marriages in which *men* list financial support as one of their top five emotional needs and their wives truly have no such need. These marriages can be quite satisfactory as long as (1) the couples go into marriage with the clear understanding that the woman will be the primary breadwinner, and (2) she has no aversion to supporting him. Couples can and do function well with a reversal of traditional roles. If a woman does have a hidden need for financial support, however, an aversion to supporting her husband may later creep into her thinking, and eventually she may find her marriage frustrating and unfulfilling.

When a woman has a need for financial support, she expects her husband's income to support her and their children, while her income is available to pay for gifts, vacations, luxury items, and other extras. This expectation is rarely explained, and many men think their career-oriented wives want to split the household expenses. In a moment of abandon, however, women will sometimes explain to their husbands that they did not expect to divide expenses. Then they often apologize for being selfish and go back to dividing expenses. They continue to be uncomfortable with that arrangement, however, because one of their most important emotional needs is not being met.

A sensible way to approach this problem is to begin with an analysis of how existing financial resources are being allocated. If a husband's income is sufficient to support his wife and family, the problem may be solved by simply dedicating his salary to pay for the family's basic needs. He gets credit for providing financial support, and that's the end of it. But if his income is insufficient to meet basic needs, then cutting household expenses may be necessary, or a change in job or career may be warranted.

I've designed a form to help couples with this analysis, the **Financial Support Inventory: Needs and Wants Budget**. Every household should have a budget, but this budget is a little different than others you've seen: It helps clarify the need for financial support. It's assumed that the spouse with this need—very likely, the wife—will find fulfillment when her definition of financial support is met.

The spouse with the unmet emotional need of financial support completes this inventory. Under the heading Needs Budget, the family's most basic living expenses are calculated and totaled. If that total is less than or equal to her spouse's income, then, by definition, her need has been met all along: She simply didn't recognize that his income was supporting her. If, however, his income is insufficient, then there are at least two solutions to the problem: (1) reduce household expenses while still meeting her basic needs, or (2) increase his income with a raise at work, a job change, or a career change.

To help document a strategy to meet this need, I've designed the form **Strategy to Meet the Need of Financial Support**. The spouse with the responsibility for providing financial support—traditionally, the husband—fills out this form. When his plan to meet his spouse's need for financial support is completed, a new Needs Budget should reflect the success of that plan. In other words, after his wife completes the Needs Budget again, his income should cover the family's basic living expenses.

While the Needs Budget is the primary focus of the inventory, the other two budgets are also very useful. The Wants Budget reflects the cost of meeting reasonable desires that would be more costly than necessities. In this column, the income of both spouses should appear. The Affordable Budget column helps you identify the wants you can afford, and will be determined by the sum of both incomes. This Affordable Budget is balanced: The income equals the expenses.

I'll make one final point on this subject. You and your spouse should agree on career choices and finances before you make any final decisions (read chapters 8 and 9 in *Love Busters*). You'll find that your wisest decisions will reflect a willingness to meet each other's needs and preferences. One of you may have no desire for added furniture, while the other is deeply troubled with what you have. Solutions recognize that while you cannot have everything you want, you can usually have the things that are most important to each of you. A certain item may not be important to both of you, but because it meets a need for one of you, the other can be genuinely enthusiastic about it and make an effort to accommodate that need. That's what happens in great marriages.

Note: You may need multiple copies of these forms, so be sure to photocopy them rather than writing in the book.

Financial Support Inventory: Needs and Wants Budget

This budget is designed to help clarify the need for financial support. The spouse with this need is to complete this questionnaire.

Please create three budgets in the spaces provided under the three columns. Under the Needs Budget column, indicate the monthly cost of meeting the necessities of your life, items you would be uncomfortable without. In the Income section, only your spouse's income should appear in the column.

Under the Wants Budget column, indicate the cost of meeting your needs and your wants—reasonable desires that would be more costly than necessities. These desires should be as realistic as possible. They should not include a new house, a new car, or luxuries unless you have been wanting these items for some time. Both your income and your spouse's income should appear in this column.

The Affordable Budget column should include all the Needs amounts and only the Wants amounts that can be covered by you and your spouse's income. In other words, your income should equal your expenses, and the Income Minus Expenses item at the end of the Affordable Budget column should be zero. This Affordable Budget should be used to guide your household finances if both you and your spouse have agreed to the amounts listed.

Payments from the past few months (or year if possible) will help you arrive at correct estimates. Use monthly averages for items that are not paid monthly, such as repairs, vacations, and gifts. Some items, such as your mortgage payment, will be the same amount for both your Needs and Wants budgets. Other items, such as vacation expense, will be much more a Want than a Need. It is highly recommended that you include in your Needs Budget an emergency expense item that is 10 percent of your total budget. In months with no emergency expenses, it should be saved for the future. Most households suffer needless financial stress when they fail to budget for inevitable emergencies. If you can think of other significant expenses, include these in the blank spaces provided.

If your spouse's income is equal to or greater than the total expenses in the Needs Budget column, it's sufficient to pay for your Needs, and it's meeting your need for financial support. It may actually be covering some of your Wants as well. That may not have been obvious, since you have not been dividing your bills into Needs and Wants. Your need for financial support is still being met when your income is used to pay for Wants that are not covered by your spouse's income.

However, if your spouse's income is insufficient to pay for your Needs, either you must reduce your household expenses without sacrificing your basic needs, or he must increase his income with a pay raise, a new job, or a new career to meet these needs.

Household Expenses and Income	Needs Budget	Wants Budget	Affordable Budget
Expenses			
Taxes			
Income tax	_____	_____	_____
Property tax	_____	_____	_____
Other taxes	_____	_____	_____
Interest			
Mortgage interest	_____	_____	_____
Credit card interest	_____	_____	_____
Automobile loan interest	_____	_____	_____
Other interest	_____	_____	_____
Insurance			
Homeowner's insurance	_____	_____	_____
Life insurance	_____	_____	_____
Liability insurance	_____	_____	_____
Auto insurance	_____	_____	_____
Medical and dental insurance	_____	_____	_____
Other insurance	_____	_____	_____
Home Expenses			
Home repair	_____	_____	_____
Home remodeling	_____	_____	_____
Home security	_____	_____	_____
Home cleaning	_____	_____	_____
Yard maintenance	_____	_____	_____
Fuel (gas and electricity)	_____	_____	_____
Telephone	_____	_____	_____
Garbage removal	_____	_____	_____
Other home expenses	_____	_____	_____
Furniture and appliances	_____	_____	_____
Furniture purchase	_____	_____	_____
Appliance purchase	_____	_____	_____
Furniture and appliance repair	_____	_____	_____

Household Expenses and Income	Needs Budget	Wants Budget	Affordable Budget
Automobiles			
Husband's auto depreciation	_____	_____	_____
Husband's auto fuel	_____	_____	_____
Husband's auto maintenance	_____	_____	_____
Wife's auto depreciation	_____	_____	_____
Wife's auto fuel	_____	_____	_____
Wife's auto maintenance	_____	_____	_____
Other auto expenses	_____	_____	_____
Food and Entertainment			
Groceries	_____	_____	_____
Dining out	_____	_____	_____
Vacation	_____	_____	_____
Recreational boat expense	_____	_____	_____
Photography	_____	_____	_____
Magazines and newspapers	_____	_____	_____
Cable TV	_____	_____	_____
Other food and entertainment	_____	_____	_____
Health			
Medical (over insurance)	_____	_____	_____
Dental (over insurance)	_____	_____	_____
Nonprescription drugs	_____	_____	_____
Exercise expense	_____	_____	_____
Special diet expense	_____	_____	_____
Other health expenses	_____	_____	_____
Clothing			
Husband's clothing purchases	_____	_____	_____
Wife's clothing purchases	_____	_____	_____
Children's clothing purchases	_____	_____	_____
Dry cleaning	_____	_____	_____
Alterations and repairs	_____	_____	_____
Other clothing expenses	_____	_____	_____

Household Expenses and Income	Needs Budget	Wants Budget	Affordable Budget
Personal			
Husband's allowance	_____	_____	_____
Wife's allowance	_____	_____	_____
Children's allowances	_____	_____	_____
Gifts			
Religious contributions (tithe, religious organizations)	_____	_____	_____
Nonreligious contributions (other charitable causes)	_____	_____	_____
Gifts for special events (birthdays, Christmas, etc.)	_____	_____	_____
Pets			
Pet food	_____	_____	_____
Veterinary expenses	_____	_____	_____
Other pet expenses	_____	_____	_____
Savings			
Savings for children's education	_____	_____	_____
Savings for retirement (IRAs)	_____	_____	_____
Savings for other projects	_____	_____	_____
Other Household Expenses			
Banking	_____	_____	_____
Legal	_____	_____	_____
Accounting and tax preparation	_____	_____	_____
Emergency fund (10%)	_____	_____	_____
_____	_____	_____	_____
Total Household Expenses	_____	_____	_____

Household Expenses and Income	Needs Budget	Wants Budget	Affordable Budget
Income			
Husband's salary	_____	_____	_____
Husband's other income	_____	_____	_____
Wife's salary	_____	_____	_____
Wife's other income	_____	_____	_____
Investment income	_____	_____	_____
Interest income	_____	_____	_____
_____	_____	_____	_____
Total Household Income	_____	_____	_____
Income Minus Expenses	_____	_____	_____

Strategy to Meet the Need of Financial Support

This form is designed to help you create a strategy to meet your spouse's need for financial support. Complete each section of the worksheet to provide yourself with documentation of the process you used to select a strategy.

1. After your spouse completes the **Financial Support Inventory: Needs and Wants Budget**, list expense items and their amounts from the Needs Budget that you may be able to reduce without sacrificing your spouse's basic needs.

   _____

   _____

   _____

   _____

   _____

   _____

   _____

   _____

   _____

2. Describe your plan to reduce these amounts. Be certain that this plan is made with the enthusiastic agreement of both you and your spouse. Include a deadline to determine if these reductions are possible.

   _____

   _____

   _____

   _____

   _____

   _____

   _____

   _____

   _____

3. If your plan to reduce basic living expenses does not succeed within your designated time limit, describe a plan to increase your income. You may wish to design several plans in succession, such as (1) asking for a raise, and if that fails, (2) changing jobs, and if that fails, (3) preparing for a higher paying career. Be certain that this plan is made with the enthusiastic agreement of both you and your spouse. Include a deadline to complete each part of your plan.

_____

_____

_____

_____

_____

_____

_____

_____

_____

4. If your plan to increase your income does not succeed within your designated time limit, will you agree to seek professional vocational help to increase your income? How will you go about finding that help?

_____

_____

_____

_____

_____

_____

_____

_____

Learning to Meet the Need of Domestic Support

Fulfillment of the male need for domestic support has fallen on the shoulders of women for thousands of years in essentially all cultures. But lately a groundswell of change has threatened fulfillment of that need in countless households. It's gotten to a point where domestic support is associated with slavery! As a result, men have been encouraged to repress this need, and a great opportunity to deposit love units is being lost.

The need for domestic support exists among men who experience a great deal of pleasure and appreciation when someone manages the home so effectively that it's seen as a refuge from the stresses of life rather than yet another source of stress. Domestic support usually includes cooking, housecleaning, washing, ironing, and child care. For some men, the meeting of this need alone can create the feeling of romantic love. Many men have fallen in love with their housekeepers.

In spite of cultural barriers to the fulfillment of this need, I encourage you to consider domestic support if your spouse listed it among his (or her) top five emotional needs. In chapter 10 of *His Needs, Her Needs*, I discuss this need and suggest a way to meet it. The approach I take is to help a couple put effort into behavior that is appreciated the most.

The first step in meeting the need for domestic support is to identify your household responsibilities (including child care). The **Household Responsibilities Inventory** is a form that helps you (1) name each responsibility, (2) describe what must be done and when it needs to be accomplished, and (3) rates its importance to both spouses.

The second step is to assume responsibility for household tasks that you would enjoy doing or prefer doing yourself. Use the **His Household Responsibilities** and **Her Household Responsibilities** forms to transfer items from the **Household Responsibilities Inventory**. After completing the transfer, you will have three lists of household responsibilities: (1) the husband's list, (2) the wife's list, and (3) the list that has yet to be assigned. This third list is made up of responsibilities that neither of you want to do, but at least one of you thinks should be done.

The third step is to assign the remaining responsibilities found on the third list to the spouse giving each item the highest importance rating. This is a fair division of labor because it assigns responsibility according to willingness and according to who benefits the most with their accomplishment. Now you have only two lists of household responsibilities—the husband's list and the wife's list.

The fourth and final step in meeting the need for domestic support raises the fair division of labor to a level that actually meets the emotional need. You may not be willing to take responsibility for a certain task because you don't think it needs to be done. But if your spouse thinks it needs to be done, it may be an opportunity for you to make massive Love Bank deposits.

Beside the name of each task on the husband's list and the wife's list, write a number indicating how many love units would be deposited if your spouse would do that task for you, or would help you with it. Use a scale from 0 to 5, with 0 indicating no pleasure and 5 indicating maximum pleasure and eternal gratitude.

If your spouse has a need for domestic support, whenever you complete a task rated 4–5 by your spouse, you may be able to deposit enough love units to sustain, or even create, your spouse's love for you. Your spouse's response to such help should prove whether or not love units are really being deposited. If your spouse thanks you when you perform these tasks and expresses his or her appreciation with affection, you know you have made the right decision. But if your spouse ignores you after you perform one of these tasks, go back to your spouse's list of tasks and pick another task that might have a greater positive impact.

As a reminder, be sure that you accomplish tasks for your spouse in ways that are not burdensome for you. If depositing love units in your spouse's Love Bank withdraws them in yours, you have not gained anything for your relationship as a whole.

Note: You may need multiple copies of these forms, so be sure to photocopy them rather than writing in the book.

Household Responsibilities Inventory

This form is designed to help you identify all your household responsibilities. But before you use this form, the husband and wife are to carry a pad of paper with them for a few days, writing down as many household responsibilities as possible when they think about them or do them. Include the name of the responsibility, a brief description of what must be done, and when it should be accomplished.

After you have both made lists of household responsibilities, make as many copies of this form as you need to include all of the household responsibilities on both of your lists. Put your combined list in alphabetical order on this form to help you eliminate duplicates. In addition to naming and describing each household responsibility, also indicate how important each responsibility is to you by giving it a rating from 0 to 5, with 0 indicating no importance and 5 indicating most important.

Task	Description	His Rating	Her Rating

His Household Responsibilities

Husbands: From your completed **Household Responsibilities Inventory**, select items that you are willing to take full responsibility for all by yourself. Then, assign to your list each of the remaining items from the Household Responsibilities Inventory where you have given it the highest importance rating. Your wife will do the same with her worksheet.

After all items from the **Household Responsibilities Inventory** have been assigned to either your list or your wife's list, then rate each item on how much pleasure you would experience if your wife would do that task for you. Use a scale from 0 to 5, with 0 indicating that you would experience no pleasure and 5 indicating that you would be eternally grateful. Also indicate with an H or C if you would simply appreciate help or if you would appreciate your wife completely taking over the task.

This form will provide both of you with valuable information as to how you can deposit the most love units by meeting each other's need for domestic support. Don't waste your energy on items of lesser importance. Put your energy where it counts most—where it means the most to your spouse.

Task	Description	Rating

Her Household Responsibilities

Wives: From your completed **Household Responsibilities Inventory**, select items that you are willing to take full responsibility for all by yourself. Then, assign to your list each of the remaining items from the **Household Responsibilities Inventory** where you have given it the highest importance rating. Your husband will do the same on his worksheet.

After all items from the **Household Responsibilities Inventory** have been assigned to either your list or your husband's list, then rate each item on how much pleasure you would experience if your husband would do that task for you. Use a scale from 0 to 5, with 0 indicating that you would experience no pleasure and 5 indicating that you would be eternally grateful. Also indicate with an H or C if you would simply appreciate help or if you would appreciate your husband completely taking over the task.

This form will provide both of you with valuable information as to how you can deposit the most love units by meeting each other's need for domestic support. Don't waste your energy on items of lesser importance. Put your energy where it counts most—where it means the most to your spouse.

Task	Description	Rating

Learning to Meet the Need of Family Commitment

The vast majority of married women have a powerful instinct to create a home and have children. Above all, they want their husbands to play a decisive role in the moral and educational development of the children. I believe that there's an underlying emotional need that manifests itself in these desires, and I call that need "family commitment."

As is the case in meeting all important emotional needs, when the need for family commitment is met, most women experience tremendous pleasure. The one who meets that need gets credit for that pleasure, and love units are deposited by the truckload.

In chapter 11 of *His Needs, Her Needs*, I describe the need for family commitment and suggest a way that men can meet that need. I recommend setting aside fifteen hours each week for "quality family time." This is not "child care," where each parent individually dresses, feeds, cleans, and supervises the play of the children. Quality family time involves the entire family, especially the mother and father, working together as a cooperative unit. The purpose of this time is to create cooperation, respect, trust, honesty, and other moral values. It is also a time when the children's education can be encouraged. Suggested events include:

- Meals together as a family
- Walks and bike rides
- Attending religious services together
- Family meetings
- Playing games together
- Attending sporting events together
- Reading to the children before bedtime
- Helping children with financial planning
- Helping children with homework
- Family projects (should be enjoyable for all with no one working alone)

The main point to remember is that these activities are designed to meet your spouse's emotional need for family commitment. As valuable as they may be for your children, if they don't deposit love units in your spouse's Love Bank, they're not meeting his/her emotional need. So the plan must include assurance that these activities are achieving what you set out to achieve: pleasure for your spouse.

I have included the **Family Commitment Inventory** to help you identify the type of family participation that your spouse would appreciate the most. Your spouse is to complete this inventory. You will discover not only the activities that your spouse wants you to develop, but also those he/she wants you to avoid. Your spouse will also indicate how much time he/she would like you to set aside to meet this need.

The **Strategy to Meet the Need of Family Commitment** form is designed to help you document your plan to implement changes in your habits and activities. When you set your plan in motion, you will find the **Family Commitment Worksheet** helpful in planning and documenting quality family time. The Quality Family Time Graph is used to record the time you spend each week meeting your spouse's need for family commitment.

This is one of those needs that, when met, not only creates romantic love, but also helps ensure the successful future of your children. It's my opinion that even when neither you nor your spouse indicates a strong need for family commitment, you should still follow my recommendation to spend fifteen hours each week in quality family time. Don't follow the crowd and subject your children to the frightening consequences of parental neglect. Your happiness is bound to the happiness of your children, and the time you spend with them is of critical importance to their future and yours.

Note: You may need multiple copies of these forms, so be sure to photocopy them rather than writing in the book.

Family Commitment Inventory

This inventory is designed to help you identify ways your spouse can meet your need for family commitment (commitment of time for family education, projects, and recreation). After you read chapter 11 in *His Needs, Her Needs*, ask yourself what your spouse could do with the family that would meet your need for family commitment. The questions in this inventory will help you answer that question, but if you feel crucial information is left out, provide it on a separate sheet of paper and attach it to this inventory.

First, under the heading Habits and Activities to Create, identify the habits and activities you would appreciate the most from your spouse. Your family time will either be enjoyable or unpleasant for you, depending on those habits and activities. You will tend to have a pleasant time when your spouse (1) is consistent in training the children, (2) disciplines the children only after first reaching agreement with you, (3) plans activities with your enthusiastic agreement, (4) interprets rules fairly, and (5) avoids using anger as part of discipline. Consider these five habits as well as others that may occur to you.

Second, under the heading Habits and Activities to Avoid, identify your spouse's habits and activities with the family that you find unpleasant. Even if some of these are just the opposite of those you want him/her to create, list them anyway.

Third, try to determine the amount of time that it takes to meet your need for family commitment. I recommend fifteen hours each week, but everybody's different, and you may feel that more or less time meets your need.

Habits and Activities to Create

1. _____
   _____
   _____

2. _____
   _____
   _____

3. _____
   _____
   _____

4. _____
   _____
   _____

5. _____
   _____
   _____

Habits and Activities to Avoid

1. _____
   _____
   _____

2. _____
   _____
   _____

3. _____
   _____
   _____

4. _____
   _____
   _____

5. _____
   _____
   _____

How much time would you like your spouse to set aside each week to meet your need for family commitment?

_____ hours each week.

Strategy to Meet the Need of Family Commitment

· ·

This form is designed to help you create a strategy to meet your spouse's need for family commitment. Complete each section of the worksheet to provide yourself with documentation of the process you used to select a strategy.

· ·

1. After your spouse has completed the **Family Commitment Inventory**, describe the habits and activities that your spouse would like you to learn.

   _____

   _____

   _____

   _____

   _____

   _____

2. Describe your plan to create the behavior listed in question 1. Be certain that this plan is made with the enthusiastic agreement of both you and your spouse. Include a deadline to learn this behavior.

   _____

   _____

   _____

   _____

   _____

   _____

3. If your plan does not succeed within your designated time limit, will you agree to seek professional help to learn this behavior? How will you go about finding that help?

   _____

   _____

   _____

   _____

   _____

4. Describe the behavior that your spouse would like you to avoid.

_____

_____

_____

_____

_____

_____

5. Describe your plan to avoid the behavior listed in question 4. Be certain that this plan is made with the enthusiastic agreement of both you and your spouse. Include a deadline to avoid this behavior.

_____

_____

_____

_____

_____

_____

6. If your plan to avoid unwanted family behavior does not succeed within your designated time limit, will you agree to seek professional help to avoid this behavior? How will you go about finding that help?

_____

_____

_____

_____

_____

7. Have you agreed to set aside the amount of family time that your spouse would like? If so, how do you plan to schedule that time each week?

_____

_____

_____

_____

_____

Family Commitment Worksheet

For the Week of _____

Please report the time you spend to meet your spouse's need for family commitment. You and your spouse must be together with at least one of your children—preferably with all of them. You should engage in the habits and activities that your spouse wants you to create, and you should not engage in those she wants you to avoid.

First, schedule time for the family by completing the Planned Family Time part of this report. The total for the week should add up to fifteen hours or the number of hours you and your spouse agreed to. Then, as the week unfolds, complete the Actual Family Time part of the report. The estimate of family time actually spent depends on how each of you feels about the quality of time spent as a family. If you have spent two hours with the family, your spouse may feel that only half of the time qualified, while you may feel that the entire two hours qualified. Because of this common difference of opinion, each of you is to provide your own estimate. In the last column, the lower estimate is to be entered. If the planned activity was canceled, explain why under Actual Activities. At the end of the week, the total of the Lower Estimate column should be entered on the **Quality Family Time Graph.**

Planned Family Time

Planned Date	Planned Time (from–to)	Total Planned Time	Planned Activities

Total Time for the Week _____

Actual Family Time

Actual Activities	Her Estimate	His Estimate	Lower Estimate

Total Time for the Week _____

Quality Family Time Graph

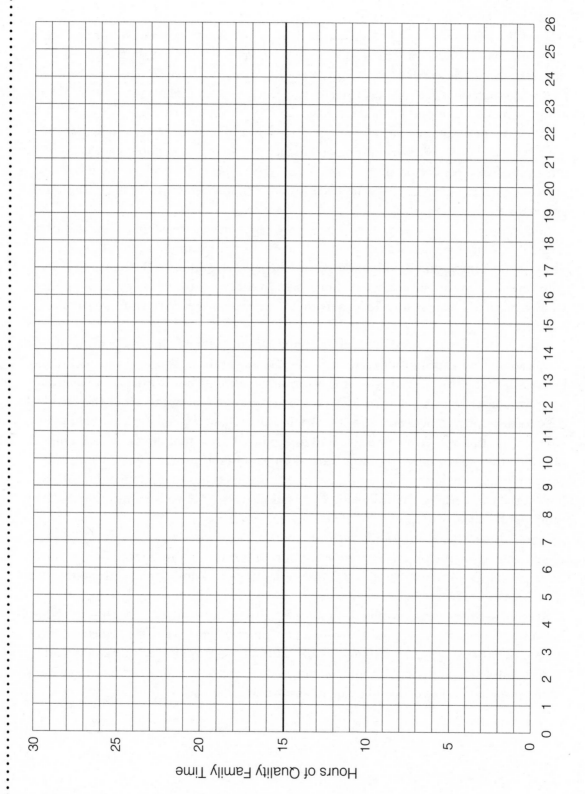

Hours of Quality Family Time

Weeks

Learning to Meet the Need of Admiration

When I list men's needs and women's needs in *His Needs, Her Needs*, I'm referring to their priority for men and women. Women also have some of the "men's needs," but they usually feel these needs are a lower priority. Men, too, have some of the "women's needs," though on a lesser level. The emotional needs with highest priority are what I consider men's needs and women's needs.

I identify the emotional need for admiration, covered in chapter 12, as a high priority need for men. But a relatively high percentage of women also chooses admiration as one of the five most important emotional needs. So with that in mind, my forms used in helping people learn to meet the need for admiration can easily apply to both men and women.

Admiration must be *honest*. It must be *felt* before it can be expressed. So one of the first steps in meeting the need for admiration is to create the feeling of admiration. When a person's most important emotional needs are being met, and Love Busters are avoided, admiration seems to follow almost effortlessly. In other words, when your spouse does what it takes to create romantic love in you, your spouse will have your admiration as a bonus.

The plan to meet the need of admiration that's outlined in chapter 12 is probably the simplest and most straightforward way to create admiration. You begin by identifying behaviors that either create or destroy your admiration. **The Admiration Inventory** helps you describe this behavior. Then you can use the **Strategy to Meet the Need of Admiration** form to help you and your spouse document a plan to create behavior in your spouse that you find admirable and to avoid behavior that destroys your admiration. Finally, you complete the **Admiration Worksheet** to provide feedback as to how your spouse is doing. In a sense, when your spouse succeeds in creating admirable behavior, the worksheet itself becomes a documented source of your admiration, thereby fulfilling the need.

If you already have admiration for your spouse, but have not learned how to express it, you should simply practice expressing your admiration more often. I've found that most people can learn to express their true feelings of admiration with just a little encouragement.

Remember that disrespectful judgments are the opposite of admiration. If your spouse has a need for admiration, he/she will be particularly sensitive to disrespectful judgments. By now, you should have eliminated all the Love Busters (step three), including disrespectful judgments, but if some remain, and your spouse has a need for admiration, focus special attention on avoiding disrespectful judgments.

Note: You may need multiple copies of these forms, so be sure to photocopy them rather than writing in the book.

Admiration Inventory

· ·

Under the heading Behavior I Admire, please name and describe the types of behavior that would help you to feel admiration for your spouse. Pay close attention to your five most important emotional needs identified in the **Emotional Needs Questionnaire** and the Love Busters identified in the **Love Busters Questionnaire**. We often admire those who are best at meeting our needs and avoid causing us unhappiness. But if your feeling of admiration seems to have little or nothing to do with your emotional needs or Love Busters, you're free to describe the behavior you admire from any perspective you wish.

If your spouse engages in behavior that tends to destroy your feelings of admiration, name and describe that behavior under the heading Behavior That Destroys My Admiration. You may find that it isn't the behavior itself that you consider inappropriate, but rather the time and place that bother you. If that's the case, explain that clearly in your description and include the appropriate circumstances under Behavior I Admire. If you need more space for your descriptions or would like to list more types of behavior than the form allows, use another sheet of paper and attach it to this form.

· ·

Behavior I Admire

1. _____
   _____
   _____

2. _____
   _____
   _____

3. _____
   _____
   _____

4. _____
   _____
   _____

5. _____
   _____
   _____

6. _____
   _____
   _____

Behavior That Destroys My Admiration

1. _____
   _____
   _____

2. _____
   _____
   _____

3. _____
   _____
   _____

4. _____
   _____
   _____

5. _____
   _____
   _____

6. _____
   _____
   _____

Strategy to Meet the Need of Admiration

This form is designed to help you create a strategy to meet your need for admiration. Complete each section of the worksheet to provide yourself with documentation of the process you used to select a strategy.

1. After your spouse completes the **Admiration Inventory**, describe behavior that your spouse admires and would like you to learn.

   _____
   _____
   _____
   _____
   _____
   _____

2. Describe your plan to learn the behavior listed in question 1. Be certain that this plan is made with the enthusiastic agreement of both you and your spouse. Include a deadline to learn this behavior.

   _____
   _____
   _____
   _____
   _____
   _____

3. If your plan does not succeed within your designated time limit, will you agree to seek professional help to learn this behavior? How will you go about finding that help?

   _____
   _____
   _____
   _____
   _____
   _____

4. Describe the behavior that tends to destroy your spouse's feelings of admiration for you.

_____

_____

_____

_____

_____

_____

5. Describe your plan to avoid the behavior listed in question 4. Be certain that this plan is made with the enthusiastic agreement of both you and your spouse. Include a deadline to avoid this behavior.

_____

_____

_____

_____

_____

_____

6. If your plan to avoid this unwanted behavior does not succeed within your designated time limit, will you agree to seek professional help to avoid this behavior? How will you go about finding that help?

_____

_____

_____

_____

_____

_____

Admiration Worksheet

• •

Please list all instances of your spouse's behavior that affect your feeling of admiration. This may be a very sensitive subject, and not all couples can objectively handle this without professional supervision. If you find your spouse emotionally upset with your honest reactions, or if you are reluctant to provide honest reactions, seek professional supervision.

• •

	Day	Date	Time	Type of Behavior and Your Reaction
1.				
2.				
3.				
4.				
5.				
6.				
7.				
8.				

Learning to Set Aside Time for Undivided Attention

A point I make repeatedly in both *Love Busters* and *His Needs, Her Needs* is that romantic love cannot be created or sustained without time for undivided attention. You don't have to be a genius to discover that unless you schedule time to meet each other's emotional needs, it won't be done.

I've included worksheets to help you organize your time so that you'll take time to meet some of each other's most important emotional needs. Setting aside time for undivided attention is one of the most difficult assignments in this workbook, not because couples object to being with each other, but because the pressures of life usually crowd out the time it takes to sustain romantic love.

During courtship, you realized that if you didn't give your boyfriend or girlfriend much time, he or she would end up with someone else. Besides, in those days you had more time. After marriage, if you are like most couples, you tend to take each other for granted and crowd each other out of your schedules. I warn you, if you don't make a special effort to give each other your undivided attention, you'll never meet each other's emotional needs, and romantic love will be impossible to sustain.

The forms I've included to help you stay on course are the **Time for Undivided Attention Worksheet** and the **Time for Undivided Attention Graph**. These are similar to the **Family Commitment Worksheet** and **Quality Family Time Graph**. And the goal is similar as well. Just as you need to set aside time to provide your family with care and guidance, you also must set aside time to meet each other's most important emotional needs.

Four emotional needs should be the primary focus of your time for undivided attention: affection, sexual fulfillment, conversation, and recreational companionship. If you fail to schedule time to give each other undivided attention, you'll neglect these extremely important needs.

The astute observer will notice that if you add the 15 hours for quality family time to the 15 hours of undivided attention, you have just committed 30 hours a week. When you add 40 to 50 hours of work, how much time does that leave? If you need about 8½ hours of sleep each night, you have about 28½ hours left (168 total hours in a week minus 59½ hours for sleeping minus 50 hours for work minus 15 hours for quality family time minus 15 hours for undivided attention equals 28½ hours). That's enough time for getting ready for work in the morning and bed at night, driving to and from work, attending church, getting enough exercise, having personal time, and engaging in other activities *if* you're organized.

But if you're not organized, don't sacrifice your marriage and family. First set aside time for undivided attention and quality family time, and make that time your highest priority. If the other things in your life are important to you, you'll learn to be a little more organized in order to fit them in.

Note: You may need multiple copies of these forms, so be sure to photocopy them rather than writing in the book.

Time for Undivided Attention Worksheet

For the Week of _____

Please report the time you give undivided attention to each other. You must be without friends, relatives, or children and must use the time to engage in conversation, affection, sex, or recreational activities that promote undivided attention.

First, schedule time to be together by completing the Planned Time Together part of this report. The total for the week should add up to fifteen hours or more. Then, as the week unfolds, complete the Actual Time Together part of the report. The estimate of time actually given to undivided attention depends on how each of you feels about the attention given. While you may have been together for two hours, one of you may feel only half of the time was given to undivided attention, while the other may feel that the entire two hours qualified. Because of this common difference of opinion, each of you is to provide your own estimate. In the last column, the lower estimate is to be entered. If the planned activity was canceled, explain why under Actual Activities.

At the end of the week, the total of the Lower Estimate column should be entered on the **Time for Undivided Attention Graph**. It should be fifteen hours or more if you want to sustain romantic love in your marriage.

Planned Time Together

Planned Date	Planned Time (from–to)	Total Planned Time	Planned Activities
____	____	____	____
____	____	____	____
____	____	____	____
____	____	____	____
____	____	____	____
____	____	____	____

Total Time for the Week _____

Actual Time Together

Actual Activities	Her Estimate	His Estimate	Lower Estimate
____	____	____	____
____	____	____	____
____	____	____	____
____	____	____	____
____	____	____	____
____	____	____	____

Total Time for the Week _____

Time for Undivided Attention Graph

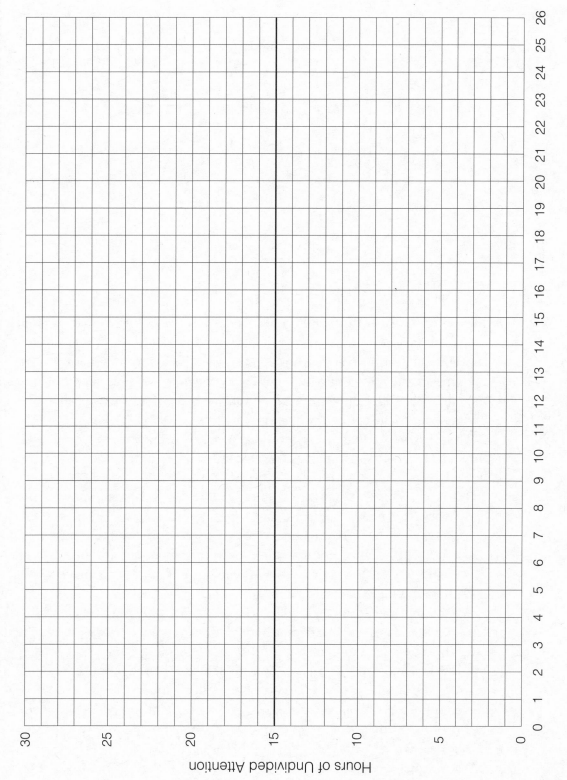

Hours of Undivided Attention

Weeks

How to Find a Good Marriage Counselor

I wrote *Five Steps to Romantic Love* to place in your hands methods and tools that have proven useful to me in saving marriages. But even the best concepts and forms won't help under certain conditions. Sometimes you need the support and motivation that only a professional marriage counselor can provide. That's why I put so much emphasis throughout this workbook on finding a marriage counselor if your own efforts fail.

The purpose of a marriage counselor, from my perspective, is to guide you through (1) emotional minefields, (2) motivational swamps, and (3) creative wildernesses.

The *emotional minefields* are the predictable yet overwhelmingly painful experiences that many couples go through as they try to adjust to each other's emotional reactions. Hurt feelings are the most common, but depression, anger, panic, paranoia, and many others seem to pop up without warning. These emotions distract couples from their goal of creating romantic love, and often sabotage the entire effort.

A good marriage counselor helps couples avoid many of these emotional landmines and is there for damage control when they're triggered. He/she does this by understanding the enormous stress couples are under as they are facing one of their greatest crises. When one or both spouses become emotionally upset, the marriage counselor has the skill to diagnose and treat the emotional reactions effectively. A good counselor knows how to calm down a couple and assure them that their emotional reactions are not a sign of hopeless incompatibility.

The *motivational swamps* are the feelings of discouragement that most couples experience. They often feel that any effort to improve their marriages is a waste of time. Over the years, I believe that one of my greatest contributions to couples has been my encouragement when things looked bleak. My clients knew that at least their counselor believed their effort would be successful. Eventually, each spouse would come to believe it too.

Discouragement is contagious. When one spouse is discouraged, the other quickly follows. Encouragement, on the other hand, is often met with skepticism by the other spouse. So it's easy to be discouraged and difficult to be encouraged when you're trying to solve marital problems. A marriage counselor can provide the realistic perspective that may be missing.

The *creative wilderness* is the typical inability of couples in marital crisis to discover solutions to their problems. In the books I've written I've suggested many solutions, but they're only the tip of the iceberg. Many marital problems require solutions that are unique to certain circumstances. In this manual, I put more emphasis on the process you should follow to solve marital problems than I do on the specific strategy you should use. That's because there are many situations that require unique strategies.

A good marriage counselor is a good strategy resource. While you can, and should, think of ways to solve your marital problems, a marriage counselor should know how to solve problems like yours. That's what you pay him or her to do! Counselors often obtain special training for common marital problems, such as sexual incompatibility and financial conflicts. These counselors can document a high rate of success in finding solutions to those problems. The strategy should make sense to you. In fact, the strategy should encourage your belief that your problems will soon be over.

To summarize, the three most important reasons to find a marriage counselor are (1) to help you avoid or overcome painful emotional reactions to the process of solving marital problems, (2) to motivate you to complete your plan to restore romantic love to your marriage, and (3) to help you think of strategies that will achieve your goal.

If you can handle your emotional reactions, provide your own motivation, and think of appropriate strategies, you don't need a marriage counselor. In fact, I suggest that you try solving your problem on your own until you hit a roadblock. But if your efforts hit a snag, find a professional marriage counselor to help you. Marital problems are too dangerous to ignore, and their solutions are too important to overlook.

How to Make Your First Appointment

The yellow pages is one of the most common places to find marriage counselors. Your physician or minister may also be able to make suggestions. The most reliable sources of referral are people who have already seen a counselor who has successfully guided them to romantic love. Since couples are usually tight-lipped about their marital problems, that kind of referral is usually difficult to obtain.

Regardless of your source of referral, however, you should take steps to be certain that you select someone who can help you. And remember, the counselor who can help your marriage helps *both* you and your spouse. If at all possible, make sure your spouse is an active participant in this selection process.

Begin by calling one clinic at a time, asking to speak to the counselor you are considering. There should be no charge for this preliminary interview. You should ask the counselor some of the following questions:

- How many years have you been a professional marriage counselor?
- What are your credentials (academic degree and state license)?
- How many couples have you counseled?
- What percentage of your clients were in love with each other at the end of therapy?
- Do you help your clients avoid some of the emotional hazards of marital adjustment?
- Do you help motivate your clients to complete the program successfully?
- Do you suggest strategies to solve your clients' marital problems?

You may wish to add other relevant questions. You may also tell the counselor what type of marital problem you have. After going through this manual, you'll probably have more insight regarding your problem than counselors are accustomed to hearing. Use that insight to discover if the counselor has the background and skill to help you with your particular problem.

I would highly recommend that you ask if the counselor is presently using my books, *His Needs, Her Needs*, *Love Busters*, and this workbook. If they are not using these materials, ask if they'd be willing to use them when counseling with you. While this may seem like a marketing ploy on my part, the reason I would like you to take my materials with you is that I'd like you to stick to the program I've recommended. There are many ineffective marriage counseling methods being used today. My direct method of dealing with the problem tends to produce positive results. Counselors that only sit and listen to couples complain should be avoided at all costs!

It's important to find a counselor who can see you right away. I've found that most couples don't go to the trouble and expense of marriage counseling for marriage "enrichment." They are in a state of crisis and facing marital disaster! Time is of the essence. You cannot wait weeks for your first appointment. In fact, you should probably be seen the same day you call.

After speaking to several marriage counselors on the telephone, and taking good notes on their answers to your questions, narrow your choice to three counselors. When you and your spouse both feel comfortable with a particular counselor, set up your first appointment. Keep all your notes, since the first one you select may not work out.

What Is the Cost?

Cost varies widely among marriage counselors. The least expensive are often available through Health Maintenance Organizations, but their overworked counselors are usually weeks away from taking new couples, and they tend to schedule follow-up appointments weeks apart. It's important that you be seen soon and often. Furthermore, HMO counselors are not likely to talk to you on the telephone prior to an appointment.

Insurance generally will not pay for marriage counseling unless the counselor finds you or your spouse suffering from a mental disorder. Treatment for the disorder through marriage counseling may be covered, however. If you see a counselor that uses your insurance, you can be almost certain that you'll be diagnosed to have a mental disorder. It'll be on your record for years to come and may prevent you from obtaining certain jobs or qualifying for certain types of insurance. Furthermore, if you really do not have a mental disorder, but it's been diagnosed just to collect insurance, your insurance company may challenge the diagnosis, and this may leave you responsible for the bill. If you're offered counseling for what your insurance pays, with no other cost to you, it's illegal. Call your insurance company or your state's insurance commissioner to report the attempt to commit insurance fraud.

It's safe to assume that you will need to pay out of your pocket for therapy. So how much do counselors charge? Rates vary from about $25 to $125 an hour. The average is about $75. Since most marriage counselors see couples one hour a week for the first three months, you will pay about $1000 in that period of time. Most of my clients have paid under $1000 by the time they've completed therapy. But some counseling can continue weekly for as long as two years before the problems have been resolved. That would cost a couple $8000 over two years. While it may seem like a fortune, the cost of divorce is often many times that figure.

To help put the cost of marriage counseling in perspective, there's nothing you can buy for $8000 that will give you the same quality of life that a healthy marriage provides. If you and your spouse love each other and meet each other's important emotional needs, you'll be able to do without many other things and still be happy in the end. Besides, I've found that people seem to earn more and save more after their marital problems are solved. The money you spend to resolve your marital problems is money well spent.

What to Expect in the First Session (Intake)

If at all possible, see a counselor in a clinic or suite of counseling offices. A receptionist should be present, and the waiting room should be pleasant and relaxing. Register at the desk when you arrive, and you'll be asked to complete registration forms and contracts. Read them carefully. You may also be asked to complete insurance forms.

Most "hour" sessions are actually fifty minutes long. Ten minutes are taken by the counselor to complete notes and prepare for the next session. While I've always tried to time my sessions carefully, I try to be flexible and considerate at the end of each hour. Sometimes, I find myself giving a couple an extra fifteen minutes to pull themselves together, putting me fifteen minutes behind for my next couple. The extra ten minutes between sessions helps me catch up when I'm running behind.

It's important that your counselor be available to begin your session at the specified time. While most counselors will occasionally run late, it should not be a pattern. Your time is important, and you shouldn't be expected to waste it waiting for your counselor. Complain if it becomes a problem.

The purpose of the first session is to familiarize yourself with the counselor. The counselor will not be able to discover how to solve your problem during the first session, but you can often determine your comfort and confidence in him or her. If you or your spouse react negatively to his or her style, find another counselor. He/she is there to inspire you, and if it doesn't happen, you'll be wasting your time. Most marriage counselors see couples together in the first session, but I do not. Instead, I see each person separately for fifteen minutes so that I can learn the perspective of each one. Besides, I've seen too many fights break out when I see couples together for the first time. For your own comfort and security, I recommend that you see your counselor separately, at least briefly, during the first session.

The counselor will ask you why you've come to see him or her, and you should answer that you've come for help in restoring love to your marriage. When you're asked to be more specific, you explain that you've both developed habits that hurt each other more than they help each other and that you want to develop more constructive habits. You want to learn to meet each other's needs and avoid being the cause of each other's unhappiness. You go on to explain that you want the counselor to help you achieve those goals.

At the end of the session, you will be asked to complete forms so that the counselor can evaluate your marital problem. I usually use a Minnesota Multiphasic Personality Inventory (MMPI), a personal history questionnaire, my Love Busters Questionnaire (LBQ), and my Emotional Needs Questionnaire (ENQ). The LBQ and ENQ are printed in this manual. To save time and provide more information, you could give the counselor copies of the forms you've already completed in this manual. If the counselor does not use forms for his evaluation, use those in this workbook to help determine your goals, strategies, and progress.

I usually try to schedule the second appointment for no more than a week later. If possible, I try to see the couple within a few days. This is because they are usually suffering from their problems and would like relief as soon as possible. I can't give them any advice after the first session because I don't know much yet. The advice comes after I've had a chance to review the forms they complete.

What to Expect in the Second Session (Assessment)

The purpose of the second session is to review the forms you've completed and plan a strategy to resolve your marital problems. It's usually impossible to do this in one hour, so you should expect this strategy session to take two or three hours.

The counselor should see you and your spouse alone for at least part of the session. As your counselor suggests his/her plan, you need to be able to react honestly, and the presence of your spouse may inhibit your reaction. At the end of the session, however, you should be together to formally agree to the plan, which is carefully described in writing. I have couples sign their agreement to the plan before they leave.

There's no point to treatment before a treatment plan is completed. Poorly organized counselors will often see clients for weeks before they get down to deciding how they'll proceed. During that time, the crisis is over and the motivation to solve the problem is postponed until the next crisis. The couple drops out of therapy no wiser or better off than when they came. To avoid that tragic end, a counselor must focus on a treatment plan immediately, while the couple is still motivated to do something about their problem.

If your counselor claims to need several sessions before arriving at a treatment plan, resist it. Explain that even if the initial plan needs to be revised during treatment, it's better to begin with some plan than no plan at all. Not only do you want to get on with it, but there's also a big risk that you or your spouse will lose motivation before the plan is completed. Most couples that come for marriage counseling need plenty of encouragement from the first session on, and it's discouraging to wait for a treatment plan. Since you come to the counselor having worked through at least part of this workbook, your goals will be much more clearly stated than they are for most couples he or she sees. For that reason, the treatment plan will be much easier to create.

At the end of the second session, you should not only know the treatment plan, but you should also be given your first assignment. The value of marriage counseling is in what you achieve between sessions, not necessarily what you achieve during the session.

One of your first assignments should be to spend and document fifteen hours when you give each other undivided attention. Most of your other assignments will be carried out during those hours. The time you set aside for each other must be carefully guarded because it's easy to let the emergencies of life crowd out your time together, leaving you without time to solve your marital problems.

You may be able to carry out the treatment plan on your own. Perhaps all you want is professional advice regarding a strategy that will help you solve the problem. If emotional minefields and motivational swamps are not a threat to your marriage, you may need the counselor's experience only to help you think of a solution to your problem that you would not have found by yourself. If that's the case, set one more appointment in a week or two to guarantee that you are carrying out the plan without any need for further help. If you're not making progress on your own, ask for more sessions with the counselor.

What to Expect During Treatment

The remaining counseling sessions will be guided by the treatment plan that you agreed to follow. Each week you report your successes and failures to the counselor. He or she guides you through the emotional minefields, motivational swamps, and creative wildernesses. If your counselor is right for you, you'll come to like and respect him/her more and more as time goes by. You'll see your marriage improve in fits and starts. Some weeks will be blissful while others will be unbearable.

It's common for couples to experience a crisis between appointments that requires a counselor's mediation. I've usually been willing to have couples call me at the office or at home for emergencies because I realize that I'm working with couples in crisis. Sometimes a call is simply for clarification of an assignment. But I've also had threats of suicide, violent arguments, and irresponsible browbeating that needed to be dealt with at the time they occurred. If I get too many calls from a couple, I schedule their appointments more closely together.

You and your spouse should determine your need for continued treatment and when to terminate treatment. I usually use the success of the treatment plan to determine how to phase clients out over time. I will see them once a week in the beginning, twice a month after they are on a steady course, and once a month when they are nearing the end. It's not uncommon for couples to return after six months or a year just to check on their status.

Men generally want to get out of therapy as soon as possible, even when they were the ones that wanted it the most in the beginning. They don't like the idea of reporting to someone regarding their behavior, and my role as a counselor is to see to it that they follow through on what they promised. They often agree to anything to get their wives back, and then once she's home, they go back to their old habits. With that type of problem in mind, don't abandon therapy unless you *both* enthusiastically agree to do so. If one of you wants to keep the door open, reschedule once a month or less often just in case problems arise.

In the end, you and your spouse will be very much in love with each other. I have couples repeat my test for romantic love every few weeks so I can be certain they're on the right track. You might want to do something similar to measure the success of your program. But when you're in love, you don't really need a test to prove it!